Men With ADHD

CRAFTED BY SKRIUWER

Copyright © 2024 by Skriuwer.

All rights reserved. No part of this book may be used or reproduced in any form whatsoever without written permission except in the case of brief quotations in critical articles or reviews.

For more information, contact : **kontakt@skriuwer.com** (www.skriuwer.com)

TABLE OF CONTENTS

CHAPTER 1: INTRODUCTION TO ADHD IN MEN

- Explains what ADHD is and how it affects men
- Describes common myths and first steps to understanding
- Highlights why some men go undiagnosed until adulthood

CHAPTER 2: HOW THE BRAIN WORKS WITH ADHD

- Breaks down key brain regions linked to attention and impulse control
- Shows how chemical signals like dopamine and norepinephrine relate to ADHD
- Explains why certain brain differences cause focus and planning problems

CHAPTER 3: EARLY SIGNS IN CHILDHOOD AND TEEN YEARS

- Looks at how ADHD can appear in very young children
- Discusses signs during middle school and high school
- Shares reasons some kids get overlooked or misdiagnosed

CHAPTER 4: COMMON STRUGGLES IN ADULTHOOD

- Reveals how inattentiveness and restlessness carry over into adult life
- Explores the effect on jobs, finances, and social duties
- Addresses issues like feeling scattered and disorganized

CHAPTER 5: DIAGNOSTIC METHODS AND EVALUATION

- Describes the process of checking for ADHD in adults
- Reviews screening tools and the role of clinical interviews
- Explains how medical checks rule out other conditions

CHAPTER 6: MEDICINES AND HOW THEY HELP

- Outlines different types of ADHD medication, including stimulants and non-stimulants
- Discusses potential benefits, side effects, and dosage factors
- Emphasizes the role of combined approaches with therapy

CHAPTER 7: THERAPY CHOICES AND HELPFUL APPROACHES

- Covers cognitive and behavioral methods for ADHD
- Explores one-on-one counseling, group therapy, and coaching
- Highlights practical tips like breaking tasks down or using rewards

CHAPTER 8: SOCIAL LIFE AND ROMANTIC RELATIONSHIPS

- Examines how ADHD affects friendships, dating, and marriage
- Shares ways to communicate better and avoid misunderstandings
- Offers advice on juggling social events and personal space

CHAPTER 9: CAREER CHALLENGES AND WORKPLACE TIPS

- Reveals common job-related struggles, like time management or impulsive actions
- Suggests scheduling tools, task blocking, and office accommodations
- Advises on balancing focus, communication, and team demands

CHAPTER 10: EDUCATION, STUDY METHODS, AND MEMORY TRICKS

- Provides strategies for men returning to school or training programs
- Suggests note-taking, test prep, and reading methods
- Explains how to manage homework, online classes, or group work

CHAPTER 11: MONEY MANAGEMENT & BUDGET TIPS

- Addresses how inattention and impulses lead to overspending or missed bills
- Recommends tools for budgeting, saving, and tracking expenses
- Explains how to handle debt and reduce financial stress

CHAPTER 12: ROUTINES, SLEEP, AND TAKING CARE OF YOURSELF

- Emphasizes the role of consistent routines in organizing daily tasks
- Covers sleep habits, meal planning, and staying active
- Shows how small steps in self-care build stability and reduce chaos

CHAPTER 13: FATHERHOOD AND FAMILY DUTIES

- Looks at parenting struggles unique to men with ADHD
- Shows how to set up routines for kids, handle emotional overload, and share duties
- Teaches ways to be present and supportive, despite focus problems

CHAPTER 14: COMMUNICATION SKILLS AND CONFLICT HANDLING

- Examines how to talk clearly and manage tense moments
- Gives tips on active listening, avoiding interruptions, and calming conflict
- Helps build better relationships through respectful dialogue

CHAPTER 15: TOOLS, APPS, AND OTHER SUPPORTS

- Lists both traditional and digital tools for planning, reminders, and focus
- Explains how to pick and use apps effectively without getting distracted
- Highlights coaching, occupational therapy, and assistive technology

CHAPTER 16: BUILDING A TRUSTED SUPPORT GROUP

- Explains why emotional backing and accountability are key
- Shows how to find or create a circle of friends, family, and mentors
- Covers professional support like therapy or workplace allies

CHAPTER 17: HANDLING SHAME, GUILT, AND MISUNDERSTANDINGS

- Talks about dealing with self-blame and external criticism
- Points out ways to see mistakes as learning opportunities
- Offers methods to reduce conflict and repair relationships

CHAPTER 18: LIFESTYLE CHANGES THAT MAKE A DIFFERENCE

- Focuses on sleep, diet, exercise, and stress control to manage ADHD
- Shows how environment and habits can lift mood and sharpen focus
- Encourages practical daily routines to keep life steady

CHAPTER 19: SORTING OUT MYTHS FROM REALITY

- Dispels popular myths about ADHD, such as it being "not real" or "only in kids"
- Provides facts to answer skeptics and handle criticism
- Encourages a scientific view that boosts confidence and reduces stigma

CHAPTER 20: SUMMARY AND ONGOING GROWTH

- Reviews main themes from diagnosis to daily success
- Recommends steady progress with new habits, therapy, and personal goals
- Encourages readers to keep adapting and refining their ADHD management over time

Chapter 1: Introduction to ADHD in Men

Overview of What ADHD Is

Attention Deficit Hyperactivity Disorder, often called ADHD, is a term used for a collection of signs that involve trouble paying attention, restlessness, and sometimes acting too quickly. People often think about children when they hear about ADHD, but men of all ages can have it. Some people learn about it only when they are adults. Others may have known since childhood. In either case, living with ADHD involves certain struggles that can look different in men compared to women.

ADHD is not just about being unable to sit still. It can affect how a person's brain handles tasks, focuses on details, and organizes thoughts. When we talk about men with ADHD, we often see patterns that can be overlooked if people think ADHD is only a childhood problem. In fact, some men do not realize they have ADHD until they start to face bigger issues at work, in relationships, or with money and day-to-day tasks.

A key point: ADHD is not caused by laziness or a lack of willpower. It is a condition that involves specific areas of the brain and the chemicals that carry signals. When a person has ADHD, it is important to know that it might require changes in habits, possible medication, or other tools to help manage it. This chapter looks at how ADHD shows up in men, why it is sometimes missed, and how it affects self-image, relationships, and careers.

A Short History of ADHD

In the past, ADHD was not always recognized. People used different names or simply said a child was hyperactive. Over time, scientists found out that there is more to it than high energy. They discovered patterns in how these individuals pay attention, process information, and react to the world around them.

In the mid-1900s, doctors began to classify problems with attention and self-control as separate conditions. They started to see that some children showed more restlessness while others struggled mostly with focus. It took many years for ADHD to be understood as involving not only kids but also adults. Today, ADHD is divided into three main types:

1. **Predominantly Inattentive Type**: This involves mostly problems with paying attention, staying on task, and following through on plans.
2. **Predominantly Hyperactive-Impulsive Type**: This involves mostly restlessness and a tendency to act before thinking.
3. **Combined Type**: This involves both inattentive and hyperactive-impulsive signs.

When it comes to men, these types can appear in ways that affect their jobs, friendships, and more. For instance, a man with predominantly inattentive type might forget important meetings and appear unorganized. Meanwhile, a man with the combined type might also show signs of fidgeting and talking out of turn.

Why Men Might Be Missed in Childhood

It may seem odd to talk about men being missed in childhood, since ADHD is often spotted in kids. However, many boys might be labeled just as "active" or "rowdy," and the idea of ADHD might not come up if teachers or parents assume that is normal boy behavior. Some parents may think the boy will simply "grow out of it," so they do not look for answers.

In addition, if a boy can focus on certain things he likes (like a favorite video game or a sport), people around him might assume he does not have trouble with attention. ADHD, though, can show up in many different ways, and a child might be able to focus intensely on something he likes, while still having big trouble focusing on tasks he does not like.

Another group of men might have done fine in school because they were clever enough to hide their difficulties. They might do okay academically but feel stressed or anxious because it takes them a lot more energy to pay attention. Later in life, when they face the challenges of a job or a family, the ADHD problems become bigger.

The Different Pressures on Men

Men often face social pressures to behave in a certain way. Society might expect men to be calm, strong, or problem-solvers. When a man finds it hard to keep his thoughts organized or gets upset easily, he might not want to admit it. Instead of seeking help, he may blame himself, thinking he is just lazy or not disciplined enough.

Men might also avoid going to a doctor for help because they do not want to be seen as weak. This can lead to long-term problems like anxiety, depression, or issues with substance use. It is vital to understand that ADHD is not a mark of personal failure. It is a real condition that doctors can help manage.

How ADHD Affects Self-Image

Many men with ADHD might think that they are not living up to expectations in various parts of life. For example, a man might fail to meet work deadlines even though he tries very hard. He might forget family events or lose important paperwork. If he does not realize he has ADHD, he might think, "I'm just not good enough."

These negative thoughts can lower self-esteem. When a person has low self-esteem, it becomes easier to give up or avoid trying. This can hurt one's sense of worth and can impact many areas, including relationships and personal health. Knowing the root cause—ADHD—can make a huge difference. It helps men see that these challenges are not because they are "bad" or "lazy," but because their brains process information differently.

Common Myths About ADHD in Men

1. **Myth**: ADHD is only a childhood problem.
   Truth: Many men have ADHD that was not identified in youth. They carry signs into adult life, affecting them at home or work.
2. **Myth**: Men with ADHD are always hyperactive.
   Truth: Some men show more of the inattentive type, with fewer signs of restlessness.

3. **Myth**: If you can focus on something, you can't have ADHD.
   Truth: People with ADHD can often focus on things that truly grab their interest. Problems arise in tasks that are boring or require sustained attention.
4. **Myth**: ADHD means a person is not smart.
   Truth: Intelligence and ADHD are not linked. Many very clever people have ADHD.
5. **Myth**: Men with ADHD just lack motivation.
   Truth: While motivation can be affected, ADHD is not about lacking the will to do things. It is about brain wiring and chemical signals.

Special Points for Men

Because men often get told to "man up" or ignore their problems, they might stuff their feelings inside or try to handle things alone. This can lead to bigger issues later. For instance, a man might overuse alcohol or other substances to cope. Or he might work extra long hours, thinking he can outrun the ADHD by brute force.

Some men with ADHD might also have sudden outbursts of anger, since frustration can build up when tasks do not get done or when simple details keep getting missed. This anger can hurt relationships. It is not that ADHD causes anger by itself, but it can set the stage for stress and emotional overload.

Hidden Effects on Daily Life

- **Difficulty Waking Up on Time**: Men with ADHD can have trouble waking up due to poor sleep routines or late nights. This can cause them to be late for work or other tasks.
- **Poor Time Awareness**: A lot of men with ADHD might not realize how much time has passed. They could think they have only spent a few minutes on a task, when in reality an hour has gone by.
- **Misplaced Items**: Losing keys, wallets, or important documents can be an everyday struggle. This can lead to arguments with roommates or partners who might feel the man is careless.

- **Messy Living Spaces**: Keeping a tidy home can be harder with ADHD. Stacks of papers, clothes on the floor, or general clutter can build up quickly.
- **Inconsistent Focus**: In one part of the day, a man might zero in on something he loves, forgetting to eat or even sleep. Then he might completely ignore tasks that do not interest him, causing deadlines to pass.

The Cost of Not Knowing

When men do not know they have ADHD, they might assume they have a personal flaw. This can lead to a cycle: they try harder, get overwhelmed, fail, and then blame themselves. Over time, they might lose hope, quit jobs frequently, or struggle in relationships. Some might end up in therapy for anxiety or depression without realizing the root cause is ADHD.

There can be financial costs too. Missing deadlines or poor budgeting can hurt a man's earnings. Job-hopping might become normal. Plus, spending money impulsively can lead to debt or big financial mistakes.

It is not just about jobs and money. Personal health can be affected. Men with ADHD might overeat, skip exercise, or ignore regular check-ups. They can get stuck in cycles of poor self-care, which increases stress.

Finding a Way Forward

It is important to know there are tools and resources. Getting a diagnosis, either from a doctor or a mental health specialist, can open doors to understanding why certain struggles have been a constant. This is often the first step. The path to diagnosis can involve:

1. **Screening Tools**: These are questionnaires that a doctor gives to see if the signs match ADHD.
2. **Interview About Background**: This includes questions about childhood, schooling, and family.
3. **Observations and Testing**: Some clinics do more in-depth testing to check attention, problem-solving, and memory.

Once a man knows he has ADHD, he can look into solutions such as medicine, therapy, and strategies for day-to-day life. This book will cover all those topics in later chapters. It is not a quick process, but knowing the reason for the challenges can offer relief and a sense of clarity.

Important Insights (Lesser-Known Facts)

- **Patterns in Sleep**: Men with ADHD might show different sleep cycles. For instance, they might find it hard to go to bed before midnight or could feel more alert at night, leading to chronic sleep problems.
- **Hormone Effects**: While hormone changes in women are often discussed, men also have hormonal shifts as they age. Testosterone levels can affect mood, and for a man with ADHD, shifts in hormones can change how strong ADHD signs feel.
- **Risk of Driving Issues**: Research shows that some people with ADHD have more car accidents or speeding tickets if they are not aware of their tendencies or do not manage them. This is not a guarantee, but a caution that impulsive actions or poor focus might carry over into driving.
- **Possible Creativity Boost**: Although ADHD can be tough, some men notice they think outside the box better than others. This can be an advantage in fields that value new ideas. Recognizing this can help a man choose a career or hobby that fits well with his brain's wiring.

How to Use This Book

The chapters ahead will explain how ADHD works in the male brain, how to get tested for it, what medicines exist, and what everyday strategies can help. We will also talk about topics like money, romance, jobs, and family responsibilities. The goal is to give specific tips and information that can be used right away. Men with ADHD can learn practical ways to manage tasks, communicate with loved ones, and keep themselves organized.

If you suspect you have ADHD or you have already been diagnosed, this book can serve as a reference. It can also be helpful for people who care about men with ADHD. Sometimes, family members or friends want to learn more so they can give support. Each chapter will add new insights, so it may help to read them in order, but you can also jump to the sections that feel most urgent.

Wrapping Up the Introduction

Men with ADHD are not alone. It might feel that way if no one else around you seems to be struggling. The fact is, many men never got help as children, and they might only learn about their condition later in life. That does not mean it is too late. Support, facts, and professional help can make all the difference. You do not have to force yourself to "just try harder." Instead, you can learn methods to handle tasks and life events more effectively.

In the next chapter, we will look more closely at how ADHD affects the brain in men. Understanding the brain differences can help clear up why certain actions or habits show up. It can also guide decisions about managing signs in daily life.

Chapter 2: How the Brain Works with ADHD

Brain Chemistry and Brain Regions

ADHD is linked to certain chemicals in the brain, mostly dopamine and norepinephrine. Dopamine is often described as a "reward" chemical, helping us feel good when we do something enjoyable. Norepinephrine helps with alertness and attention. In men with ADHD, the levels or handling of these chemicals might not work the same as in men without ADHD.

Several areas of the brain are important:

1. **Prefrontal Cortex**: This region is often called the "executive center." It is responsible for planning, organizing, and controlling impulses. In ADHD, this area can be underactive or might not communicate well with other parts of the brain.
2. **Basal Ganglia**: This area helps regulate movements and also influences how the brain processes rewards. Dopamine plays a big part here, and men with ADHD might have different activity in this region, leading to restlessness or impulsive choices.
3. **Cerebellum**: Known mainly for motor control and coordination, the cerebellum also helps in keeping attention and managing tasks. Some studies show that people with ADHD might have slight differences in how this region develops.

When these parts of the brain do not work together properly, it can create the signs we see in ADHD: trouble focusing, being impulsive, or appearing restless.

Brain Wiring and Neural Networks

Aside from separate parts of the brain, ADHD also involves how signals move along certain pathways, often called neural networks. In a well-regulated brain, signals between the prefrontal cortex, basal ganglia, and other areas move smoothly. In a brain with ADHD, these signals can be slower or might not fire in the usual patterns. This means the person might switch from one thought to another too quickly or not be able to stick with one thought.

Men with ADHD can feel like their brains are always seeking stimulation. This is partly due to differences in the reward circuits that rely on dopamine. If the brain is not getting enough dopamine from everyday tasks, the person might look for new activities that provide quick excitement. This can show up as "thrill-seeking," changing hobbies a lot, or focusing on tasks that give fast feedback.

Differences Between Adult and Child ADHD Brains

While ADHD is often first noted in childhood, the adult male brain can show different patterns as a person gets older. Childhood hyperactivity might slow down, turning into internal restlessness. A man might feel unable to relax or might always feel the urge to move on to the next thing. The inattentive signs can become more of a problem when adult responsibilities pile up. Tasks like paying bills, organizing schedules, and handling job duties require strong executive function—an area that can be weaker in ADHD.

For adults, the brain might develop some coping routes. These are ways the brain tries to overcome its own challenges. A man might learn to set multiple alarms or keep a strict routine to compensate for poor attention. These coping methods can help, but without understanding the root cause, a man might feel constant pressure to maintain these routines.

Practical Info About Brain Differences

1. **Scanning Patterns**: Some men with ADHD have a scanning way of focusing. Their eyes or thoughts bounce around a room or a screen, looking for something that seems new or exciting.

2. **Working Memory**: This is the part of memory that holds information temporarily to perform tasks. In ADHD, working memory might be lower, making it hard to do multi-step tasks in an orderly way.
3. **Response Inhibition**: The ability to stop oneself from acting on an impulse can be reduced in ADHD. For example, a man might blurt out something without thinking if his brain's response inhibition is not strong.
4. **Time Blindness**: Some men with ADHD might not sense time passing in the same way as others. This can lead to constant tardiness.

Understanding these brain-based differences helps a man with ADHD see that he is not simply lazy or forgetful on purpose. There is an actual reason behind these struggles.

The Impact of Brain Differences on Daily Life

Work

At work, a man with ADHD might find it hard to keep track of many projects at once. Even simple tasks like filing reports or filling out forms can become complicated if he loses focus. Brain differences in attention regulation can cause him to zone out during meetings, missing key points. On the other hand, he might have bursts of energy that let him work very fast for short periods, impressing coworkers but struggling to maintain that pace.

Relationships

The same brain differences that cause scattered attention at work can affect how a man interacts with friends or a spouse. He might seem disinterested if he forgets parts of conversations. He could also get easily annoyed when people do not move at his speed. Some partners of men with ADHD report feeling that they are not heard or that they have to do more tasks at home because the man loses track of them.

Finances

Money management often relies on planning, remembering due dates, and controlling impulses. With ADHD, each of these can be a problem. Men with ADHD might buy items without thinking, or forget to pay a bill, leading to penalties. They might also find budgets hard to follow, either because they do not keep track or because unplanned expenses come up due to lack of impulse control.

Social Life

Basic tasks like texting friends back or organizing a hangout can be hard to manage with ADHD. A man might forget plans or double-book events. He could also get bored easily if the conversation is not interesting, jumping to a new topic, which could seem rude. Understanding the brain-based cause can help men with ADHD explain their actions to friends, so they do not take it personally.

The Role of Neurotransmitters

Dopamine and norepinephrine are not the only chemicals involved, but they are the main ones often linked to ADHD. When we talk about ADHD medications, many of them work by increasing the amount of dopamine or norepinephrine in the brain, or by helping these chemicals last longer in the synapses (the gaps between brain cells where signals pass).

By adjusting these levels, the brain can pay better attention and control impulses. However, this does not mean medication fixes everything. It just helps create a more even "playing field" for the person's thoughts. That is why therapy, coaching, and strategies are also needed.

Brain-Based Strategies

1. Break Tasks into Pieces

Since the ADHD brain can get overwhelmed, it helps to split jobs into smaller parts. For example, if you have to clean the garage, break it into:

"Gather all boxes, move them out, decide what to keep, and then sweep the floor." By focusing on one small piece at a time, the brain can handle tasks better.

2. Use External Reminders

Because of working memory challenges, it might help to rely on lists, alarms, or apps that remind you when things need to be done. This takes pressure off the brain's internal tracking, which might not be reliable.

3. Reward Yourself

People with ADHD often respond well to rewards. Even small rewards—like a short break or a snack after completing a task—can help the brain stay motivated. This is due to how dopamine works in creating a sense of satisfaction.

4. Change Settings to Reduce Distractions

Working in a quiet room or using noise-canceling headphones can help reduce outside triggers. Some men with ADHD do well in active environments, but many need fewer distractions to focus.

5. Physical Activity

Exercise can boost the levels of dopamine and other chemicals in the brain that help with attention and mood. A short walk or a quick workout can improve focus. It can also reduce stress, which can help with emotional balance.

Lesser-Known Brain Facts

- **Default Mode Network (DMN)**: This network in the brain is active when the mind is not focused on the outside world. In ADHD, shifting from the DMN (daydream mode) to task-positive networks (focus mode) can be harder, leading to mental "drifting."

- **Reward Deficiency Syndrome**: Some experts suggest that certain people with ADHD have a "reward deficiency," meaning they need stronger or quicker rewards to feel satisfied. This might explain why some men with ADHD seek high-stimulation activities like gambling or extreme sports.
- **Different Brain Growth**: Some studies note that certain brain regions in people with ADHD may develop at a different pace. This does not mean they are less intelligent. It just means those areas might take longer to mature, resulting in prolonged issues with planning or impulse control.

The Emotional Part of the ADHD Brain

Men with ADHD might also notice that they feel emotions more strongly or shift between emotions quickly. This is sometimes called emotional dysregulation. The brain areas that handle emotional control might not filter out small irritations, causing bigger reactions. This can lead to quick flashes of anger, sadness, or excitement.

Learning to handle these emotions can involve methods like mindfulness or structured talk therapy, which will be explained in detail in later chapters. The main idea is to recognize that these strong emotions are not signs of weakness; they often stem from how the brain handles emotional signals.

Sleep and the ADHD Brain

Sleep is crucial for all humans, but men with ADHD might have a harder time getting to sleep or staying asleep. Their minds might be buzzing with thoughts at night, or they might crave stimulus right before bed. This can lead to late-night web browsing or binge-watching shows, pushing bedtime later and causing fatigue in the morning.

Lack of sleep can make ADHD signs worse. Without enough rest, the brain struggles even more with attention and impulse control. It becomes a cycle: ADHD makes it hard to sleep, poor sleep makes ADHD worse. Finding a good evening routine can help break that cycle. Some ideas include:

- Avoiding screens for at least 30 minutes before bed.

- Keeping the bedroom dim and quiet.
- Setting a consistent bedtime and wake-up time.

How Brain Knowledge Guides Treatment

When doctors or therapists know how ADHD affects the brain, they can suggest treatments that tackle those specific issues. For example, if a man has major problems with impulsive spending, therapy might focus on planning routines and using apps that block quick online purchases. If time blindness is a key issue, he might be advised to set multiple alarms or use a timer to break tasks into blocks.

Knowing these details helps pick the right type of medicine too. Some medicines boost dopamine quickly, while others give a steady release. The choice depends on how a man's ADHD shows up and how his brain responds.

Avoiding Blame

A big reason to understand the ADHD brain is to avoid self-blame. Many men think, "If I just had more willpower, I could fix this." That is like telling a person with poor eyesight to "just see better." Without glasses or contacts, they simply cannot see as well. In the same way, a man with ADHD needs the right tools and help to handle focus and impulse control.

Understanding the brain's role helps friends and family realize that the struggles are not made up. They are real differences in how the mind functions. This can lead to more patience and better support at home.

Steps to Take If You Suspect ADHD

1. **Look for More Information**: Books, articles, and reputable websites can provide guidance.
2. **Talk to a Professional**: A doctor or mental health worker can do tests or refer you to a specialist.
3. **Discuss with a Trusted Person**: Sharing concerns with a spouse, friend, or family member might help you get support.

4. **Keep Track of Patterns**: Note times when you lose focus or act impulsively. Write them down to show a doctor later.

Building on Brain Knowledge

Later chapters will talk in detail about medication, therapy methods, and daily strategies. This chapter sets the stage by explaining that ADHD is rooted in differences in how the brain develops and communicates. By knowing these differences, men with ADHD can make sense of past struggles and plan better for the future.

The next chapters will look at signs that show up in childhood and teen years, as well as common struggles men face as adults with ADHD. The more you learn, the better you can shape a management plan that fits your personal situation and brain wiring.

Chapter 3: Early Signs in Childhood and Teen Years

Why Early Signs Matter

Many people think ADHD mainly appears in childhood. This is partly true. Early signs can show up when a boy starts school or even earlier. However, it can look different in each child. Some children may be labeled as "hyper" or "daydreamers," while others might simply seem a bit disorganized or slow to finish tasks. Recognizing these signs can make a huge difference because when parents, teachers, or doctors spot them early, they can help the child build healthy habits. Even if these signs were missed, understanding them now can help a man look back on his childhood and realize that his struggles have an explanation.

Signs in Preschool and Elementary School

1. **Restlessness**: Boys with ADHD may have trouble sitting still during circle time or short lessons. Instead of focusing, they might constantly shift around, play with nearby objects, or wander off when they are supposed to remain seated.
2. **Inability to Follow Simple Directions**: In preschool or early elementary years, most kids learn to follow simple instructions like, "Put your toys in the box." A child with ADHD might get distracted halfway and move on to something else.
3. **Constant Talking or Interrupting**: Some boys will speak out of turn or interrupt adults and other kids. They might not mean to be rude; they just cannot hold back their thoughts.
4. **Trouble Waiting for Their Turn**: Whether it is waiting in line, waiting to speak, or waiting to play with a toy, the child might grow impatient very fast. This can cause conflicts with peers.
5. **Impulsiveness**: Boys might grab items they want without asking, dash outside without telling an adult, or climb on things that are not safe.

6. **Losing or Misplacing Items**: A boy might leave his lunchbox on the playground or forget to bring homework home. He might also lose jackets or shoes more than other kids.

These behaviors do not always mean a child has ADHD, but they can be warning signs, especially if they keep happening over time. Many parents notice these patterns, but they might think, "He's just active," or "He'll grow out of it." While some kids do outgrow hyperactivity, ADHD does not just disappear if it is truly there.

Middle School and Teen Years

When a boy moves into middle school, there is a shift. Classes get harder, expectations increase, and teachers might give more complex assignments. If ADHD is present, the boy might start to have bigger challenges:

1. **Falling Behind in Assignments**: Middle school teachers often expect students to keep track of multiple subjects. A boy with ADHD might forget deadlines or fail to follow multi-step homework instructions.
2. **Procrastination**: He might wait until the last minute to start projects. This can be tied to trouble planning tasks, difficulty with time management, or feeling overwhelmed.
3. **Emotional Swings**: Teens can experience bigger mood changes, and those with ADHD might have stronger reactions. They might get frustrated easily when faced with a tough assignment or respond poorly to criticism from parents or teachers.
4. **Forgetting Details**: He might do the main part of a project but leave out key points. Or he might know the material for a test but forget to bring the needed books or sheets to class.
5. **Social Clashes**: Teens with ADHD might talk too loudly or interrupt friends, causing tension. They might blurt out comments in class or act impulsively in social settings.
6. **Inconsistent Performance**: One day, the teen might do very well on a test if it catches his interest, while other days he performs poorly because he cannot force himself to focus on subjects he finds boring.

During teen years, other factors start to appear. Hormones, peer pressure, and a push toward independence all make life more complicated. If the teen has unrecognized ADHD, he might develop feelings of frustration or thoughts like, "Why can't I handle what everyone else can?" This can hurt self-esteem and lead to more negative behavior.

Hidden Warning Signs

Daydreaming and Quiet Behavior

Not all boys with ADHD run around the classroom. Some are quiet, appear to be listening, but their minds are elsewhere. They might stare at the board without really absorbing the lesson. Because they are not loud or disruptive, teachers may not notice their struggles. This type of ADHD (often the inattentive type) can go unnoticed for years.

Frequent Headaches or Stomach Aches

Sometimes stress from school or social issues can lead to physical complaints. A teen might say he has a stomachache to avoid going to school if he feels overwhelmed. Adults might think he is making excuses, not realizing the child truly feels anxious or stressed because of ADHD-related challenges.

Excessive Computer or Video Game Use

Some teens with ADHD find that games or social media give them fast feedback and constant stimulation. This can be very appealing to the ADHD brain, which often craves novelty or excitement. If a boy spends too much time on these platforms, it might be a sign that he is trying to escape tasks he finds boring or hard to focus on.

Early Signs of Risky Behavior

Impulsiveness can lead to risk-taking behaviors, such as skateboarding down steep hills without protective gear or sneaking out late at night. Not every teen with ADHD does these things, but the chance is there if impulsiveness is strong and the teen lacks healthy outlets.

The Role of Parenting and Environment

A boy's home life and the adults around him play a big part in how the early signs of ADHD develop. If parents or guardians offer consistent routines and guidance, a child might handle his ADHD better. But if there is chaos at home, the child might have more trouble.

- **Consistency**: Clear rules, regular bedtimes, and a stable homework schedule help.
- **Positive Reinforcement**: Praising effort can encourage a child to keep trying, even if he makes mistakes.
- **Understanding**: If parents realize the child is not being defiant on purpose, they can respond calmly and seek professional help.

In many cases, parents themselves might have ADHD or other conditions and not realize it. This can make it hard for them to recognize signs in their children or to provide structure.

Early Intervention

If a boy is diagnosed in childhood, he may benefit from:

1. **Medication**: Certain medicines can help balance brain chemicals and improve focus, but it should be done under the care of a doctor.
2. **Behavioral Therapy**: A therapist can teach ways to manage impulses, set goals, and develop problem-solving skills.
3. **Classroom Accommodations**: Extra test time, seating in a quiet spot, or the ability to move around can help the child learn better.
4. **Parent Training**: Parents can learn techniques to support the child's needs without resorting to anger or punishment.

With early intervention, many kids learn coping skills that they can carry into adulthood. However, an early diagnosis is not the end of the story. Even with help, ADHD can reappear in new ways as life changes.

The Teen's Perspective

Teenagers often want more freedom, which can clash with their need for structure. A teen with ADHD might:

- Resent rules if they feel controlled.
- Struggle to keep up with more challenging schoolwork.
- Argue with parents who try to enforce schedules.
- Experience shame if they cannot do what friends do easily.

Some teens try to hide their struggles by pretending they do not care about school or other responsibilities. Others might rebel more directly, leading to conflicts at home. Understanding that the teen is not acting out on purpose can ease tension. That is why communication, patience, and seeking professional help can make a real difference.

Puberty and ADHD

Hormones during puberty can affect ADHD signs. Testosterone, for example, changes how the body and brain handle stress and excitement. A teen with ADHD might notice shifts in mood, motivation, or impulse control. This can make the teen years even more unpredictable. For parents and teachers, it is important to recognize that sudden changes in behavior might not just be "teen drama." It could be ADHD reacting to these biological changes.

School Issues and Teacher Reactions

Teachers might notice a boy who:

- Never has the required materials.
- Forgets to do homework or loses it.
- Speaks out without raising his hand.
- Appears to know the material but flunks tests due to silly mistakes.

Some teachers are very supportive and might suggest an evaluation for ADHD. Others might see the boy as lazy or disobedient. This difference in teacher response can shape how the boy feels about school. If he is lucky enough to have a teacher who understands, he might get the help he needs early. If not, he might keep struggling and develop a dislike for school.

Transition to High School

High school is a jump in academic difficulty. Classes last longer, workload is heavier, and social pressure increases. A boy with ADHD might:

- Miss key deadlines for big projects.
- Feel lost in large classrooms.
- Have trouble meeting extracurricular demands.
- Experience bullying or social isolation due to impulsive actions.

On the flipside, if he finds a sports team or club that taps into his energy and interests, he might shine. For example, a student with ADHD might excel in a drama club because it provides immediate feedback and excitement. Another might do well in robotics club if it keeps him mentally engaged.

Emotional Challenges

A teen with ADHD often faces emotions he cannot fully explain. He may worry about his future. He might feel embarrassed if he has to take medication at school. Some might compare themselves to classmates who seem to manage responsibilities more smoothly. Feelings of shame or low self-confidence can arise.

In some cases, teens might seek comfort in unhealthy coping methods. This can include overeating, substance use, or hanging out with peers who encourage reckless behavior. That is why spotting these patterns early and guiding them toward healthier alternatives is key.

When ADHD Goes Undiagnosed

A boy might graduate high school (or drop out) never knowing he has ADHD. During those years, he might develop negative labels about himself:

"I'm dumb," "I'm lazy," or "I can't do anything right." Without proper help, he might step into adulthood with these beliefs, which can affect his relationships, work, and overall well-being. This sets the stage for more struggles down the road.

Lesser-Known Factors in Childhood and Teen ADHD

- **Sleep Disorders**: Children with ADHD are more prone to sleep problems, such as restless leg syndrome or disrupted sleep cycles, which can worsen daytime focus.
- **Learning Differences**: Some boys have both ADHD and a specific learning difference, such as dyslexia. This can complicate how they do in school and might make signs of ADHD more or less obvious.
- **Overfocusing on Interests**: While ADHD often involves poor attention, many children can focus very hard on things that fascinate them (like video games or a certain hobby). This intense focus might mislead adults into thinking the child does not have ADHD.
- **Physical Symptoms**: Chronic headaches, stress rashes, or stomach troubles can appear if the child is constantly anxious about school or home tasks.

Helping Teens Prepare for Adulthood

Even if a teen is not formally diagnosed, parents and adults can do a few things to help him build skills:

1. **Organization Tools**: Teach him to keep a planner, use phone reminders, and break large tasks into small steps.
2. **Positive Activities**: Encourage interests like sports, music, or other hobbies that provide constructive outlets.
3. **Communication Skills**: Show him how to express his thoughts calmly and listen to others without interrupting.
4. **Time Management**: Help him set small goals, like finishing a certain number of tasks before taking a break.

5. **Professional Guidance**: If possible, seek an evaluation. A formal diagnosis can open doors to extra school support and possible medication.

Conclusion of Chapter 3

Childhood and teen years are prime times for ADHD to become noticeable, but it is often misunderstood. Signs can range from restlessness to quiet inattention, making it easy for some kids to slip through the cracks. Social pressures, changing hormones, and bigger school demands mean that a teen with ADHD can face many challenges, especially if the condition remains hidden. Understanding these early indicators is crucial, both for the teen himself and for the adults who guide him.

Recognizing these signs can save years of confusion and allow for healthy development of coping skills. With the right support, many children and teens learn how to channel their energy, keep track of tasks, and head into adulthood with more confidence.

Chapter 4: Common Struggles in Adulthood

Why Adult ADHD Matters

While ADHD is commonly linked to children, it does not vanish when they turn 18. Men can carry signs into adulthood, facing hurdles in work, personal life, and health. If it was never identified in their youth, they might have no idea why tasks that seem easy for others feel like a mountain for them. Recognizing these adult struggles is the first step toward change. Understanding that ADHD can continue past teen years helps break the illusion that it is solely a kid's issue.

Work and Career Challenges

1. **Trouble with Organization**: Adult jobs often require keeping track of multiple projects, answering emails on time, or following a detailed schedule. A man with ADHD might create piles of papers on his desk or miss important messages because his inbox is overflowing.
2. **Poor Time Management**: Many adults with ADHD show up late to meetings or procrastinate on tasks. This might cause friction with bosses or colleagues who view punctuality as crucial.
3. **Difficulty Following Through**: Starting tasks can be easy if they are exciting. Finishing them is the real hurdle. Men with ADHD might leave projects half-done when they lose interest or become distracted by something else.
4. **Impulsive Decisions**: In certain jobs, impulsiveness can cause serious errors. For instance, sending out an email without proofreading or making quick financial calls without careful thought.
5. **Job Hopping**: Some men switch jobs often because each new role feels fresh at first. Once boredom sets in, they might seek a different position. This can hamper long-term career growth and income stability.

Personal and Family Life

Romantic Relationships

- **Communication Gaps**: Men with ADHD might forget important details, like a partner's requests or plans. This can lead to arguments when the partner feels ignored or unimportant.
- **Emotional Flare-Ups**: If a man is frustrated at work or with himself, he might snap at his partner without warning. Later, he may regret it, but the damage is done.
- **Inconsistent Support**: On a good day, he may be very caring and attentive. On a bad day, he might seem distant or lost in his own world.

Parenting

If a man with ADHD has children, he might face additional strains:

- **Difficulty Keeping a Routine**: Kids thrive on structure, but the father might struggle to maintain set meal times, bedtime routines, or consistent discipline.
- **Forgetting Tasks**: He might forget to pack his child's lunch or show up late to a parent-teacher conference. Over time, this can strain the relationship with both the child and the school.
- **Impulsive Reactions**: Small mistakes by the child might trigger a bigger reaction than intended because the father is already stressed.

Social Circles

Friends might be understanding at first but can grow tired of last-minute cancellations, late arrivals, or the feeling that the man is not listening during conversations. Over time, some friends may distance themselves. This leads to loneliness, which can worsen other ADHD-related issues like anxiety or depression.

Money and Finances

Money management is a notable problem for many adults with ADHD. Difficulties can include:

1. **Impulse Spending**: A man might purchase items on a whim—new gadgets, clothes, or even bigger expenses—without thinking it through.
2. **Late Bills**: He may forget due dates, leading to late fees and a damaged credit score.
3. **Poor Record-Keeping**: Trying to keep receipts and bank statements in order can feel overwhelming, increasing the chance of overdrafts or missed payments.
4. **Budgeting Issues**: Even if he writes a budget, sticking to it can be tough if he loses track of daily spending.

Over time, financial stress can build up, feeding into anxiety and relationship conflicts. Some men realize they are in deep debt and cannot recall exactly how it happened. Recognizing ADHD as a factor can encourage them to seek financial tools and advice that match their attention challenges.

Emotional Health Problems

Adults with ADHD often face other emotional or mental health issues. Some common ones include:

- **Anxiety**: Constant worry about unfinished tasks, late deadlines, or forgetting key details can fuel anxiety.
- **Depression**: Feelings of guilt or shame for not measuring up to what society or family expects can spiral into hopelessness.
- **Anger and Irritability**: Frustration about repeated mistakes or feeling misunderstood can cause a short fuse.
- **Substance Use**: Some men might turn to alcohol or other substances to cope with stress or restlessness.

These issues can mask or worsen ADHD signs. For example, if a man is depressed, he might struggle even more to focus and could withdraw socially. Sometimes, treating ADHD can also ease these other conditions, but each issue might need its own approach.

Daily Life Difficulties

Housekeeping

A man with ADHD might find it hard to keep his home in order. Dirty dishes can pile up, laundry might remain unfolded for days, and clutter can build. He may try to straighten up, only to get distracted midway. This can be frustrating if he shares the living space with a partner or roommates who prefer cleanliness.

Scheduling and Calendars

Planning doctor's appointments, kids' activities, and errands can be overwhelming. The adult with ADHD might forget to write things down or forget to check the calendar. This can lead to double-booking or missing appointments. Some men rely heavily on their partners to manage schedules, which can cause tension if the partner feels overburdened.

Nutrition and Exercise

Cooking balanced meals and sticking to an exercise routine both take planning and discipline. Adults with ADHD might skip meals or grab fast food because it is faster. They might join a gym in an excited burst of motivation, only to stop going after a few weeks.

Unique Struggles for Older Men

As men age, the effects of ADHD might shift. Some men find that hyperactivity lessens, but forgetfulness and time management remain big issues. If a man has worked the same job for a long time, he might have routines that help him get by. Once retirement or major life changes happen, he may suddenly face new schedules or responsibilities. These can bring ADHD back to the forefront if he no longer has a structured environment.

Physical health concerns might also emerge. If an older man has high blood pressure or heart problems, certain ADHD medicines might not be recommended. This can leave him seeking different ways to handle focus and energy issues. Also, older men might face hearing or vision changes that increase confusion if they already have attention problems.

Social Pressures

Men, in many cultures, are expected to be providers and stay in control. If a man's ADHD causes mistakes at work, financial trouble, or general disorganization, he might feel he is failing in his role. This can lead him to hide his struggles, putting on a front that everything is fine. Over time, keeping up this act is exhausting. Some men may avoid seeking help due to fear of being judged as weak or incompetent.

Workplace Issues That Might Be Overlooked

- **Difficulty Keeping Up with Email**: In a modern office, email is crucial. A man with ADHD might have an inbox with hundreds of unread messages because each email demands attention, and he feels overwhelmed.
- **Forgetting Verbal Instructions**: If a boss or coworker gives directions orally, the man might nod along, only to realize later he cannot recall half of what was said.
- **Struggle with Repetitive Tasks**: Some jobs involve tedious data entry or other tasks that do not vary. Adults with ADHD might do these tasks poorly, looking for any excuse to move on to something else.

Anger and Conflict

A repeated theme is the frustration that can build up when a man tries very hard but sees little improvement. Misunderstandings with family or coworkers can lead to fights, which then feed back into shame or anger. For example, if a man forgets his wedding anniversary, his spouse might interpret it as not caring. He might lash out in defense, thinking, "I really tried to remember, but it just slipped my mind." Such tensions can be minimized when both sides understand ADHD's effect.

Unique Information: The Role of Stimuli

Adults with ADHD might feel more at ease in high-stimulation settings. Some men do better at jobs that involve movement or quick decisions, such as construction or emergency services. They might excel when there is just enough excitement to hold their attention. However, this can become a double-edged sword if they get too much stimulation and become overwhelmed, or if the job has slow periods where they get bored and lose focus.

Avoiding the Trap of Self-Blame

Many adult men think, "I should have grown out of this by now," or "I'm just not disciplined." That mindset can create a cycle of guilt. Realizing there is a neurological factor helps break that cycle. It does not remove personal responsibility for actions, but it shows that these challenges have a root cause in how the brain works. With proper help—through medication, coaching, therapy, or practical tools—adults can adapt.

Balancing Family, Work, and Personal Life

Men with ADHD often find it difficult to balance multiple parts of life. They might pour too much focus into one area, like work, and neglect family and self-care. Or they might spend a lot of time on a new hobby, ignoring job obligations. Learning to create boundaries and schedules is critical. For instance:

- **Setting timers** for tasks at work so they do not go on forever.
- **Marking family events** on a calendar that is checked every morning.
- **Planning self-care** time, such as 30 minutes for a short walk or reading a book, to avoid burnout.

Coping with Adult Education or Career Change

Some adults return to school for higher education or change careers in their 30s, 40s, or beyond. ADHD can pose challenges with heavy reading loads, complex projects, or the need to network with new people. The man might feel like he is back in middle school, forgetting deadlines or skipping important details in essays. Colleges often have disability resource centers that can provide help, such as extended test time or note-taking assistance. Seeking these accommodations can be the difference between success and failure.

Tech and Tools

Modern technology offers many tools that can help an adult with ADHD:

1. **Task Management Apps**: These apps can break tasks into smaller steps, send reminders, and track progress.
2. **Calendar Alerts**: Digital calendars can sync with phones and computers, giving audio or pop-up alerts before important events.
3. **Voice Assistants**: Devices like smart speakers can be asked to set timers, reminders, or even help create a shopping list.
4. **Email Filters**: Setting up rules that automatically sort emails into folders can reduce inbox chaos.

However, too many apps can become distracting if the user tries to juggle them all. The best approach is to pick a few reliable tools and use them consistently.

Self-Advocacy at Work

If a man suspects ADHD is affecting his performance, he might choose to talk with a supervisor or human resources (HR) representative. This is a personal decision, as not all workplaces are equally supportive. But in some places, adjusting certain aspects of the job—like allowing more flexible break times or providing a quieter workspace—can greatly help. Knowing what to ask for is important, and it helps if the man has ideas ready, such as:

- "Could I have a desk farther from the busy hallway?"
- "Is it possible to break large projects into smaller deadlines?"
- "Could I get instructions in email form as well as verbally?"

Male Pride and Struggles with Diagnosis

Some men avoid official evaluations because they fear being labeled. They might also worry about insurance or job implications. Yet, an evaluation can confirm that ADHD is real, not just a personal failing. This can unlock options like medication or therapy. With the right approach, it is possible to handle the condition in a way that does not harm one's career.

Unique Insights for Men

- **Aggressive Driving**: Some adult men with ADHD admit to more aggressive or risky driving habits, driven by impulsivity or boredom on the road.
- **Relationship Guilt**: Repeatedly forgetting special days or household tasks can cause deep guilt. Knowing ADHD's role can help a man address the problem with strategies, like placing calendar reminders.
- **Overcommitting**: Adults with ADHD might get excited about opportunities and say "yes" to too many. Then they get overwhelmed or have to back out, leading to disappointment or frustration.

Strategies to Ease Common Adult Problems

1. **Set Realistic Goals**: Break long-term objectives into small steps. Instead of "I must get in shape this year," try "I will exercise twice a week for 20 minutes each time this month."

2. **Use Visual Aids**: Sticky notes, color-coded files, or big wall calendars can serve as constant reminders of tasks and due dates.
3. **Peer or Friend Support**: Find a buddy who can check in regularly, either a friend, a colleague, or a support group member. This can keep a man accountable.
4. **Plan for Downtime**: Because the ADHD mind can get overloaded, scheduling short rest periods or fun activities can help prevent burnout.
5. **Regular Health Check-Ups**: Physical and mental health often go hand in hand. Staying on top of blood pressure, cholesterol, and mental health screenings can catch problems early.

Summary of Adult Struggles

Men with ADHD face real hurdles in various parts of life: work, personal relationships, finances, and beyond. Some might have suspected ADHD for a while, while others might stumble upon it after years of confusion. Acknowledging that these struggles are not just a result of poor character can bring relief and open the door to effective solutions.

Key Takeaways:

- Work demands can clash with the ADHD tendency toward disorganization and impulsiveness.
- Personal relationships might suffer if a man does not have strategies to manage memory lapses and mood swings.
- Financial problems can build due to poor impulse control and missed deadlines.
- Emotional health issues, like anxiety or depression, often appear alongside ADHD, making daily life harder.
- Tools and supports, from medication to workplace accommodations, can help men handle these challenges.

The next chapters will explore topics such as getting diagnosed, exploring treatment, and building specific approaches to handle daily tasks. Armed with a clearer view of the adult ADHD experience, men can move toward managing their signs in a healthy, productive way.

Chapter 5: Diagnostic Methods and Evaluation

Introduction

Many men spend years grappling with attention problems, impulsive behavior, and disorganization without knowing why. They might think they are just lacking motivation or that they must push themselves harder. In reality, there can be an underlying cause: ADHD. Figuring out that ADHD is the reason can be a huge relief, because then real solutions can be found.

This chapter focuses on how experts determine if someone has ADHD. It outlines the common methods used, including questionnaires, interviews, and medical checks. It also clarifies who does these evaluations—doctors, psychologists, psychiatrists, or specialized therapists. By learning about these diagnostic methods, men can approach the process with more confidence and get a reliable answer.

Some men fear getting a formal evaluation, worried they will be labeled or judged. But an accurate diagnosis can help them get support. In many cases, a diagnosis confirms what a person has felt for years—that life tasks are harder than they should be. Once the problem is named, it is much easier to find ways to solve it.

Why Diagnosis Is Important

Better Understanding of Personal Struggles

A diagnosis provides a clear explanation for repeated difficulties. If a man cannot hold a job or maintain an organized life, he might blame himself. But if a professional says, "You have ADHD," that shifts the perspective. It is not about laziness; it is about how the brain is wired. This new understanding can reduce guilt and shame.

Access to Proper Support

Without a formal diagnosis, it can be harder to get help in academic or work settings. Many employers and colleges have policies that allow some considerations, like extra time on tests or help with time management, but these are often only given when there is documentation. A clear diagnosis can open the door to these resources.

Tailored Treatment Plans

Treatment for ADHD can include medication, therapy, coaching, and lifestyle changes. But every person's symptoms are different. A formal diagnosis highlights a person's specific problem areas (inattention, restlessness, or impulsivity). From there, a doctor can suggest what might be most helpful. For instance, a man with mostly inattentive signs might benefit a lot from memory aids, while someone with big impulse issues might focus more on strategies that slow down quick decisions.

Reducing Other Risks

Undiagnosed ADHD can lead to frustration, relationship conflicts, and low self-confidence. It can also overlap with depression or anxiety. Identifying ADHD early can prevent or reduce these problems, since proper management can lessen life's stress.

The Professional Team: Who Is Involved in Diagnosis?

Several types of professionals might be part of an ADHD evaluation:

1. **Primary Care Doctors (Family Doctors)**: Some people start by talking to their regular doctor. While these doctors can do initial screenings, they might refer the patient to a specialist for a more thorough check.
2. **Psychiatrists**: These are medical doctors who specialize in mental health. They can diagnose conditions, prescribe medication, and monitor how the patient responds.

3. **Psychologists**: They usually hold a doctoral degree in psychology. They cannot prescribe medication in most regions (though rules differ by location), but they can do detailed assessments that include behavior tests, questionnaires, and interviews.
4. **Neuropsychologists**: These professionals specialize in the link between brain function and behavior. They might run specific tests to measure attention, memory, and other cognitive skills.
5. **Therapists and Counselors**: While they might not diagnose ADHD on their own, they can play a role in identifying possible signs and guiding a person to seek a formal evaluation.
6. **Occupational Therapists or Educational Specialists**: Sometimes these professionals, especially in a school or vocational setting, notice signs of ADHD. They can suggest an evaluation but usually do not give a formal diagnosis.

In most cases, the best approach is a combination. A psychologist or psychiatrist might do specialized tests, then the primary care doctor might monitor overall health. A counselor could offer therapy sessions to handle emotional effects. Working together, these experts can form a complete picture of a man's strengths and weaknesses.

Criteria and Tools for Diagnosis

The DSM Guidelines

In many countries, professionals use a guide called the Diagnostic and Statistical Manual of Mental Disorders (DSM). It outlines specific signs that must be present for a diagnosis of ADHD. These include:

- Inattention signs (for example, failing to pay close attention to details, trouble holding focus, forgetfulness, disorganization).
- Hyperactivity/impulsivity signs (for example, fidgeting, leaving a seat when staying seated is expected, talking too much, blurting out answers, difficulty waiting).

A person must have a certain number of these signs, and they must have started before age 12. They also have to cause problems in multiple settings—work, social life, or at home. However, many adults do not recall if these signs started exactly before 12, so professionals usually piece together clues from school records, family interviews, or personal memories.

Standardized Questionnaires

Professionals often use questionnaires to check if someone meets the criteria for ADHD. Examples include:

- **ADHD Self-Report Scale (ASRS)**: A short survey that asks about things like daydreaming, forgetting tasks, or feeling restless. It is frequently given to adults.
- **Conners' Rating Scales**: There are versions for adults, teachers, and parents. Although used more often with children, it can help gather past information.
- **Barkley Adult ADHD Rating Scale**: This covers behaviors linked to executive function, time management, and focus.

These tools help professionals see patterns. They are not perfect on their own, but they give a structured way to see if signs match ADHD.

Interviews

Interviews are key. A professional might spend an hour or more talking with a patient about daily life, past experiences in school or jobs, family relationships, and personal habits. The person might say things like, "I was always the kid who got up in the middle of class," or, "I often lose track of what I am doing halfway through." These real-life examples provide evidence for how ADHD might affect them.

The interviewer may also speak with close family members or friends. Sometimes, an adult might not fully remember what his behavior was like as a child, but a parent or sibling can fill in details. Partners might describe the adult's current struggles with planning or impulsivity.

Observations

While not always possible for adults, some clinics do observations. They might watch how the person behaves in a waiting room or how he performs tasks in an office setting. If the person seems easily distracted by small noises or cannot sit still, these observations back up the findings from questionnaires and interviews.

Step-by-Step Evaluation Process

1. **Initial Screening**: The individual might take a brief questionnaire at a doctor's office or mention concerns about focus and memory. If the results suggest ADHD, the doctor recommends a thorough evaluation.
2. **Health Check**: The doctor may do a physical exam or order basic blood tests to rule out other medical issues. Low thyroid function, sleep disorders, or certain vitamin deficiencies can mimic ADHD-like signs.
3. **Detailed Interview**: This is where the professional asks about childhood, teen years, and current problems. They may also explore family history, since ADHD can run in families.
4. **Questionnaire Completion**: The person fills out one or more formal rating scales. Sometimes family members or a partner do a companion form to offer another viewpoint.
5. **Other Tests**: Some clinics use computer-based attention tests. For example, the T.O.V.A. (Test of Variables of Attention) measures how well a person can stay focused over a set period. These tests are not always used, but they can provide extra data.
6. **Review of Records**: If possible, the professional checks old school records, standardized test scores, or job performance reviews. These might show a pattern of inattention or impulse issues over many years.
7. **Feedback Session**: After collecting all the information, the professional shares the results. If ADHD criteria are met, they discuss treatment options. If not, they might look into other explanations like anxiety, depression, or learning differences.
8. **Planning**: The last step is creating a plan. This might involve medication, therapy, or coaching. The professional might also refer the person to other specialists, like a counselor or dietitian, if needed.

Additional Medical Tests or Approaches

Some people wonder if brain scans or genetic tests can diagnose ADHD. At the moment, there is no single brain scan or blood test that says, "Yes, this is ADHD." Brain imaging research shows some patterns related to ADHD, but these are not yet used for routine diagnosis. Instead, experts rely on clinical evaluations, rating scales, and personal histories.

That said, a doctor might order tests like a sleep study if they suspect sleep apnea is causing problems. If the person has severe headaches, they might do an MRI to rule out other issues. But these are to exclude other conditions, not to confirm ADHD itself.

Overlapping Disorders and Misdiagnosis

Anxiety and Depression

Many adults with ADHD also have anxiety or depression. A man might feel anxious because he is always behind on tasks, or he might become depressed after years of feeling like he cannot measure up. During an evaluation, doctors check if these other conditions are present and whether they are separate issues or results of ADHD. Treating the root problem can often improve anxiety or depression.

Learning Differences

Some men have learning differences, like dyslexia or dyscalculia, in addition to ADHD. If the man had problems with reading, writing, or math, these might have been misunderstood as attention issues. A thorough evaluation can tease out which struggles come from ADHD and which come from other causes.

Substance Use

If a man has used alcohol or drugs to handle his restlessness or frustration, it might mask or worsen ADHD. Some substances can temporarily make a person feel more focused, while others increase impulsive behaviors.

Evaluators must be aware of the role substance use might play in clouding the picture.

Personality Issues

People sometimes confuse ADHD with certain personality features. For example, someone who is bold or rebellious might seem impulsive, but that does not always equal ADHD. A detailed evaluation helps differentiate between personality traits and true ADHD signs.

Myths About ADHD Diagnosis

1. **Myth**: If you did well in school, you can't have ADHD.
   Fact: Some men with ADHD do well academically, especially in early years if they are bright or if the material interests them. Problems may show up in college or work when tasks are not as interesting.
2. **Myth**: Professionals hand out ADHD diagnoses too quickly.
   Fact: In reality, a good evaluation takes time. Most professionals do not label someone with ADHD without a careful assessment of symptoms, history, and current functioning.
3. **Myth**: Only people with major hyperactivity need an evaluation.
   Fact: The inattentive type of ADHD can be just as serious, even if the person is not loud or restless. Diagnosis can help both forms.
4. **Myth**: A single test can confirm ADHD.
   Fact: There is no quick test for ADHD. The process involves multiple steps, from questionnaires to interviews and medical checks.
5. **Myth**: You must have a chaotic childhood record to be diagnosed.
   Fact: Some men did not have major school trouble, or their families might not have realized the signs. If the signs were present but overlooked, an adult diagnosis is still valid.

Lesser-Known Facts That Can Help

- **Age of Diagnosis**: While many think ADHD is caught in childhood, it is not uncommon for men to be diagnosed in their 30s, 40s, or beyond.

- **Cultural Differences**: In some cultures, restlessness or forgetting tasks might be blamed on "bad behavior" or "lack of discipline," leading to missed ADHD diagnoses.
- **Combination of Types**: Some men shift between inattentive and hyperactive patterns over time, depending on life circumstances.
- **Executive Function**: This term refers to the set of mental skills that include planning, following steps, and controlling impulses. Problems with executive function are a big piece of ADHD and are central to diagnosis.

What Happens After Diagnosis

If the diagnosis is ADHD, the professional will likely suggest treatment, which can include:

- Medication (stimulants or non-stimulants)
- Behavioral therapy or coaching
- Lifestyle adjustments, like better sleep schedules or exercise
- Support from support groups or online forums

Many find that a combination of medication and behavioral strategies works best. Some men might not need or want medication right away. Others might try medication and see quick improvement in focus and mood. Either way, the goal is to make daily life less overwhelming and more manageable.

Facing the Fear of Evaluation

A lot of men hesitate before going for an ADHD evaluation, worried they might be labeled or that the results might affect their job. But the information from a diagnosis is private health data. It is up to the individual whether or not to share it with an employer. In most places, employers cannot discriminate based on a medical condition.

Another reason some men avoid evaluation is that they do not want to seem "weak." But ADHD is not a weakness in character; it is about how the brain works. A man who seeks help shows strength by addressing a real issue. In fact, many discover that getting diagnosed makes them feel understood and hopeful for the first time in a while.

Questions to Ask During Evaluation

- "What type of ADHD do you think I might have?"
- "Do I have any overlapping conditions like anxiety or depression?"
- "What treatment options do you recommend?"
- "How can I manage my daily tasks while waiting for treatment to work?"
- "What resources or reading materials would help me learn more?"

Taking notes or having a trusted friend or family member come along can help. It is easy to forget questions or get nervous during a doctor's visit.

The Impact of a Good Diagnosis

A proper diagnosis can explain years of confusion. It can open doors to better job performance, more stable relationships, and improved self-confidence. Rather than feeling stuck or blaming oneself, a man can see that there is a real reason behind his struggles, and that solutions exist.

People sometimes worry a diagnosis will define them. But in reality, it is just a label for a set of signs. Men with ADHD still have unique personalities, strengths, and interests. The label helps them understand what is going on so they can move forward.

Chapter 6: Medicines and How They Help

Introduction

When men think about ADHD treatment, they often picture medication first. Medicines do play a big part in managing ADHD for many adults, but they are not the only option. However, for those who do need medicine, it can be a game-changer. Suddenly, tasks that used to feel impossible become more doable.

Medication for ADHD usually targets certain brain chemicals, especially dopamine and norepinephrine, which are related to attention, motivation, and impulse control. This chapter provides a detailed look at the types of medicines used, how they work, and what side effects to watch out for. It also addresses common myths and questions about taking medication as an adult with ADHD.

Why Medication?

Quick Boost for Attention

Some men benefit from medication because it gives a noticeable increase in their ability to focus. This can be especially useful at work or in college, where meeting deadlines and keeping attention on repetitive tasks is vital.

Better Control of Impulses

Impulsivity—speaking out of turn, making hasty decisions, or feeling restless—can get in the way of daily life. Medicines can help slow down that internal motor, allowing a moment to think before acting.

Reduced Emotional Swings

Although ADHD medication is not designed for mood disorders, better focus can reduce stress. Feeling more in control of tasks can lead to calmer emotions. Some men notice they snap at their families less or feel less anxious when they have medication support.

Combined with Other Treatments

Medication often works best when used together with therapy, coaching, or other supports. For instance, a man might use medicine to calm his mind enough to follow strategies in therapy sessions.

Types of ADHD Medicines

Stimulants

Overview: Stimulants are the most common and well-known treatment for ADHD. They increase levels of dopamine and norepinephrine in the brain, making it easier to focus and control impulses.

Examples:

- Methylphenidate (available under different brand and generic names)
- Amphetamine-based medicines (various brand names and generics)

How They Work: Stimulants help the brain's signal pathways work more efficiently. They do not create new chemicals; they help the brain use what is there. This can help the person stay on task, reduce fidgeting, and handle daily activities better.

Short-Acting vs. Long-Acting:

- **Short-Acting**: These usually last around 4 hours. A man might need multiple doses in a day.
- **Long-Acting (Extended Release)**: These can last 8-12 hours, which might cover a work or school day in one dose.

Side Effects:

- Loss of appetite
- Trouble sleeping if taken too late in the day
- Headaches or stomachaches
- Increased heart rate or blood pressure
- Irritability when the medicine wears off

People have different reactions. One man might do well on a low dose, while another needs a higher dose or a different type. Close monitoring by a doctor helps find the right balance.

Non-Stimulants

Overview: Non-stimulant medicines are an option for those who do not respond well to stimulants or who have conditions that make stimulants risky (for example, certain heart issues). They usually affect norepinephrine more than dopamine.

Examples:

- Atomoxetine: Primarily boosts norepinephrine levels.
- Certain blood pressure medicines (like guanfacine or clonidine) sometimes used in ADHD, though they were originally meant for hypertension.

How They Work: Non-stimulants often take longer to have an effect. Some men notice changes only after a few weeks. Because of their different chemical action, they may not give the same quick focus boost as stimulants, but they can still help with overall attention and impulsiveness.

Side Effects:

- Sleepiness or fatigue
- Nausea
- Dry mouth
- Possible changes in blood pressure
- Sexual side effects in some cases

Non-stimulants can be helpful for men who experience strong side effects from stimulants or who have issues with anxiety that might worsen under stimulant use.

Myths and Misunderstandings About ADHD Medication

1. **Myth**: Medicines turn people into robots.
   Reality: When dosed correctly, medication can help a man become more himself, not less. He may actually feel more engaged in activities because his focus is better.
2. **Myth**: Stimulants always cause addiction.
   Reality: When used under a doctor's supervision and taken as prescribed, ADHD medication has a low risk of addiction. In fact, some men find they are less likely to abuse substances once their ADHD is treated.
3. **Myth**: Only children should take ADHD medication.
   Reality: Adults with ADHD can benefit just as much, if not more, given that their daily obligations—jobs, families—can be demanding.
4. **Myth**: You must stay on medication forever once you start.
   Reality: Treatment plans vary. Some men use medication for specific periods, like during demanding work projects or college, and then reduce or stop under doctor guidance. Others find ongoing use helps them remain stable.
5. **Myth**: Taking medication is cheating or being weak.
   Reality: Medication is a tool. People wear glasses to see better or take insulin for diabetes. ADHD medication is just another medical support, not a crutch or an unfair advantage.

How Doctors Decide Which Medication Is Right

Every man's body and brain chemistry are different. A doctor looks at:

- **Medical History**: Heart problems, high blood pressure, or a history of substance use might guide the choice of medication.

- **Past Response to Medicines**: If someone took a certain stimulant in childhood and had bad side effects, the doctor might try a different one.
- **Daily Schedule**: If the man needs to focus in the morning more than in the evening, a short-acting dose might help. If he works long hours, a long-acting form might be better.
- **Lifestyle Factors**: Sleep schedule, diet, exercise habits, and stress level can affect how someone responds to a medicine.

Doctors often start with a low dose and slowly increase it. This allows them to watch for side effects and find the point at which focus improves without major drawbacks. Adjusting the dose or switching medicines is common in the early phases.

Practical Tips for Using ADHD Medication

1. **Take It at the Same Time Daily**: Consistency helps maintain a steady level in the body and makes side effects more predictable.
2. **Watch for Changes in Appetite**: Men might need to plan healthy meals or snacks when they are most hungry if the medicine reduces appetite at typical meal times.
3. **Monitor Sleep**: If the medicine causes insomnia, try taking it earlier or talk to the doctor about a lower dose or different type.
4. **Keep Tabs on Side Effects**: Write down any headaches, mood changes, or other issues. Discuss them at follow-up appointments so adjustments can be made.
5. **Avoid Extra Caffeine**: Both stimulants and caffeine can boost heart rate and jitteriness. Reducing coffee or energy drinks can help control side effects.

The Role of Health Checks

Before and while taking ADHD medication, doctors might:

- **Check Blood Pressure and Heart Rate**: Especially if the patient is on stimulants.
- **Monitor Weight**: Some men lose weight due to reduced appetite.

- **Ask About Mood**: Medication can affect mood, so the doctor might screen for anxiety or depression.
- **Discuss Any Substance Use**: Combining certain medicines with alcohol or other substances can be risky.

Regular check-ups help ensure the medicine is still helpful and that no harmful side effects are creeping in.

Medication and Co-Occurring Conditions

Many men with ADHD also deal with anxiety, depression, or other challenges. In these cases, doctors might prescribe a different type of medicine or combine medicines. For example, a man with both ADHD and anxiety might do better with a non-stimulant, because some stimulants can increase nervousness. Or the doctor might add an anti-anxiety medicine if the ADHD medication alone does not help enough with stress.

Lesser-Known Points About ADHD Medication

- **Medication Holidays**: Some men take breaks on weekends or vacations to reduce side effects or allow appetite to return. This should only be done with a doctor's guidance, as sudden changes can cause mood swings or other issues.
- **Genetics and Metabolism**: Not everyone processes medication the same way. Some break down stimulants quickly, needing higher or more frequent doses. Others feel overstimulated at a low dose.
- **Brand vs. Generic**: Some men find they react differently to generic versions of stimulants than to brand-name ones, even though the active ingredient is the same. The fillers or release mechanism can vary.
- **Long-Term Effects**: Studies show that when used properly, ADHD medication is generally safe. However, it is still important to have periodic reviews with a doctor to see if the benefits continue to outweigh any risks.

Alternatives to Medication

Though this chapter focuses on medicine, it is worth mentioning other approaches:

- **Therapy and Coaching**: Behavior therapy can help men learn to plan tasks, manage time, and handle emotional surges. Coaching can give step-by-step strategies to stay organized.
- **Lifestyle Changes**: Regular exercise, good sleep, and a balanced diet can support brain health. Some men find that certain foods (like those high in protein) help them focus better.
- **Mindfulness and Stress Reduction**: Techniques such as simple breathing exercises can train the mind to stay present, reducing the scatter effect of ADHD.

These alternatives are often used alongside medicine, but some men manage ADHD without medication if their signs are mild or if they respond especially well to non-medical strategies.

Talking to a Doctor About Medication

When meeting with a doctor:

1. **Share Your Full Medical History**: Mention any other health conditions, past surgeries, and all current medicines or supplements.
2. **Explain Your Symptoms Clearly**: Let the doctor know if your main problem is focus, impulsivity, restlessness, or a mix.
3. **Ask About Side Effects**: Find out what to watch for and when to call the doctor.
4. **Discuss Follow-Up**: Ask how often you should come back to tweak the dose or evaluate progress.
5. **Voice Any Worries**: If you are worried about addiction, cost, or long-term effects, say so. The doctor can clear up misunderstandings or give advice on cost-saving options.

Cost and Insurance

Medication can be expensive, depending on insurance coverage and whether the drug is brand-name or generic. Some insurance plans require trying a generic first before covering a brand name. Others may need an approval process where the doctor justifies why a specific medication is necessary. It is wise to check with your insurance provider and ask your doctor about lower-cost options.

If you do not have insurance, certain clinics or discount programs might help cut costs. Some medication makers have assistance programs if you meet specific income guidelines. Pharmacies also sometimes offer discount cards. It helps to do research or speak with a social worker to learn about local resources.

Managing Possible Side Effects

It is normal to feel a bit anxious about side effects. Some of the ways men handle them include:

- **Insomnia**: Take the medicine earlier, or ask the doctor about switching to a shorter-acting form. In some cases, a mild sleep aid might be used temporarily.
- **Reduced Appetite**: Try eating a full breakfast before taking the medication. Have snacks ready for when hunger does return. Focus on nutrient-rich foods to make the most of smaller meals.
- **Irritability**: Sometimes adjusting the dose helps. In other cases, short therapy sessions can teach ways to calm down when frustration strikes.
- **Upset Stomach**: Taking medication with food or choosing a different type can relieve this problem.
- **Headaches**: Drinking enough water and avoiding too much caffeine can help. If headaches persist, talking to the doctor is important.

Personal Responsibility and Common Sense

While ADHD medication can be very helpful, it is not magic. The person still needs to set alarms, use planners, and work on better habits. The medicine makes these habits easier to maintain because it improves focus and cuts down on the internal noise. But success still involves effort.

Men also need to use common sense about timing and dosage. Overusing medication or ignoring doctor instructions can lead to more side effects or potentially dangerous situations (like high blood pressure). Keeping track of how you feel each day and reporting back to the doctor is key.

Success Stories

Many men find that once they start the right medication, they see an immediate change in their ability to complete tasks. They may finish work projects on time, keep track of bills, or hold calm conversations with their loved ones. Others see more gradual improvements. Either way, the relief that comes from feeling more in control of one's mind is significant.

However, not everyone sees dramatic results. Some men discover that the benefits are small or that side effects are too strong. This is why a good partnership with the doctor is crucial. Adjusting dosage or switching medicines is part of the normal process of finding the best option.

Chapter 7: Therapy Choices and Helpful Approaches

Introduction

Medication can help many men with ADHD, but it is not the only way to improve focus or reduce impulsivity. Therapy approaches offer a structured path to deal with thoughts, behavior, and emotional ups and downs. This chapter looks at common therapy methods, their pros and cons, and some useful techniques you can start using right away. Whether you already take medication or choose not to, these therapy approaches can be key in handling ADHD day by day.

Therapy is not only for mental health problems like depression or anxiety. It can also help with managing daily tasks, improving self-image, and forming better habits. A good therapist can guide you through practical exercises—like making a simple checklist or practicing short calming methods when stress hits. Over time, small changes add up to a more balanced, less chaotic life.

Types of Therapy

1. Cognitive Behavioral Therapy (CBT)

Overview: CBT is one of the most studied forms of therapy for ADHD. It focuses on how thoughts affect feelings and actions. If a man constantly thinks, "I always mess things up," he might feel discouraged and act less effectively. CBT teaches how to spot unhelpful thoughts and replace them with more realistic ones. For example, "I made a mistake, but I can try a different method next time."

How CBT Helps ADHD:

- **Breaking Tasks into Steps**: CBT sessions often include learning to divide goals into smaller parts.

- **Recognizing Thought Traps**: A man might notice that he jumps to negative conclusions whenever he forgets something at work.
- **Building Healthy Routines**: By practicing new thinking patterns, a person becomes more likely to follow through on daily habits, like checking a to-do list each morning.

Typical Length: CBT can last anywhere from a few weeks to several months. Men often notice benefits within a short period if they do the homework assignments consistently.

2. Behavioral Therapy

Overview: This approach looks at actions and tries to modify them through a reward-and-consequence framework. It is often used with kids, but adults can benefit too. A man might set up a system where he rewards himself with a relaxing activity after completing a challenging task, or he might enlist a friend to keep him accountable for daily responsibilities.

How Behavioral Therapy Helps:

- **Clear Goals**: You pick specific behaviors to improve, such as reducing lateness, finishing tasks on time, or cutting back on interrupting people.
- **Tracking Progress**: You keep records (possibly on paper or in an app) of each time you successfully do or do not do the chosen behavior.
- **Rewards and Adjustments**: You celebrate successes with small treats or rest periods. If the behavior does not improve, you adjust the plan.

For adults, the key is to choose real-life rewards that are meaningful, such as time to work on a favorite hobby or enjoying a special meal. This helps reinforce good habits.

3. Interpersonal Therapy (IPT)

Overview: IPT focuses on relationships and communication. If a man with ADHD struggles to maintain stable interactions with family, friends, or coworkers, IPT can help him learn to handle disagreements, set healthy boundaries, and read social cues more effectively.

How IPT Helps:

- **Communication Drills**: The therapist might role-play certain scenarios, like bringing up a concern at work or apologizing to a friend for a missed appointment.
- **Building Empathy**: Understanding others' viewpoints can reduce social tension.
- **Managing Conflict**: Learning ways to express frustration without snapping or shutting down.

4. Coaching for ADHD

Overview: An ADHD coach is not exactly a therapist; rather, they specialize in practical methods for daily organization, time management, and goal-setting. The coach and client often speak by phone or video chat, but some do meet in person. Coaching can be short-term or long-term.

How Coaching Helps:

- **Weekly Check-Ins**: The coach helps set tasks for the week. Then, they see what worked or failed at the next check-in.
- **Accountability**: Knowing you have someone to report to can push you to meet deadlines or stick to routines.
- **Personalized Tips**: The coach might show you how to use a planner effectively, set alarms on your phone, or arrange your workspace so things are easier to find.

ADHD coaching is often more direct and skill-based compared to general therapy. It zeroes in on practical issues like scheduling, budgeting, or balancing household duties.

5. Mindfulness-Based Approaches

Overview: Mindfulness training involves learning to pay attention to the present moment without judgment. For men with ADHD, the mind often leaps from one thought to another. Mindfulness techniques, such as simple breathing exercises, encourage a calmer, more aware mental state.

How Mindfulness Helps:

- **Reducing Impulses**: By pausing and noticing an urge before acting on it, you gain a moment to choose your response.
- **Lowering Stress**: Regular practice can ease anxiety, which often appears alongside ADHD.
- **Boosting Self-Awareness**: You learn to spot when your mind starts drifting or racing, and then gently bring it back to the present.

Some therapists mix mindfulness methods into their sessions, and there are also mindfulness apps or classes you can try on your own.

Finding the Right Therapist

Credentials

Look for therapists who have experience with adult ADHD. They might be psychologists, licensed counselors, or social workers. Sometimes psychiatrists also offer therapy, although many mainly handle medication. Credentials like "Licensed Professional Counselor (LPC)" or "Licensed Clinical Social Worker (LCSW)" can be indicators of qualified therapists.

Approach and Style

Each therapist has a different style. Some are more structured, assigning homework and worksheets each session. Others prefer a free-flowing discussion. It might take a few visits to see if a particular style works for you.

Cost and Insurance

Therapy can be costly. Check if your insurance covers mental health services, and find out if there are limits on the number of sessions. Some clinics use a sliding scale based on income. If money is tight, you can ask local mental health centers about low-cost options or see if online therapy might be cheaper.

Building Trust

A good therapist should be non-judgmental, understanding, and knowledgeable about ADHD. If you do not feel comfortable after a few sessions, it might be wise to look for someone else. Having a supportive, respectful connection is key to progress.

Techniques You Can Use at Home

Therapy goes beyond the hour you spend in a session. Below are a few techniques you can practice at home to boost focus and handle impulsivity:

1. **The 5-Minute Rule**: If a task seems huge, commit to working on it for just 5 minutes. Often, once you start, you keep going. This helps sidestep procrastination.
2. **Time Blocking**: Set specific blocks of time for tasks (e.g., 30 minutes for email, 15 minutes for a quick chore). Use a timer. When the block ends, take a short break or switch tasks. This creates structure that can keep your mind from wandering.
3. **Reward Charts**: List important tasks for the week on a chart and mark them off when finished. Treat yourself to something small but pleasant after a set number of tasks. This mirrors behavioral therapy concepts and can be done without a therapist if you prefer.
4. **Pause-Before-Speaking**: Practice taking one slow breath before responding to someone. This small delay can prevent blurting out comments or interrupting. It also gives you time to form a clearer thought.
5. **Mindful Breaks**: Set an alarm once or twice a day to take a 2-minute "quiet pause." Close your eyes, breathe gently, and notice any tension in your body. This simple exercise can reset your mind and reduce restlessness.

Addressing Emotional Needs

Men with ADHD can struggle with self-worth, shame, or anxiety. Therapy can help with these emotional challenges by providing a space to talk openly. Many men grow up hearing they should be tough or deal with problems alone. In reality, discussing these feelings can reduce the weight they carry and improve overall well-being.

Anger and Frustration

Impulsivity can lead to outbursts. Therapy can show you how to spot early signs of anger—racing heart, clenched jaw—so you can cool down before exploding. Techniques like counting to ten, leaving the room for a moment, or redirecting your focus can gradually become second nature.

Shame and Guilt

Repeated mistakes—forgetting appointments, losing jobs, or missing deadlines—can lead to feeling incompetent. Therapy works to separate the condition from the person's worth. You learn it is not about being "broken"; it is about having a brain that needs different strategies. Shifting that mindset can ease guilt and promote healthy self-respect.

Relationship Strains

If ADHD has led to conflict at home, couples therapy or family therapy could help. A trained professional can teach better communication, show how to set up shared routines, and help both partners understand each other's needs. This often reduces tension that builds when one partner feels like they always have to pick up the slack.

Group Therapy and Support Groups

Sometimes, men find it helpful to join a group with others who have ADHD. These can be led by a professional (group therapy) or be peer-led support groups. Benefits include:

- **Sharing Ideas**: Members often exchange tips for managing everyday tasks.
- **Feeling Less Alone**: Hearing that others face the same issues can be reassuring.
- **Building Accountability**: Group members may check in with each other about goals.

However, group therapy might be overwhelming if the environment feels chaotic or if participants repeatedly interrupt each other. It depends on how well the group is structured. Some groups hold sessions online, which might work better for men with busy schedules or limited local resources.

Online Therapy Options

With internet use growing, online therapy has become more common. This can be through video calls, phone calls, or even text-based apps. Advantages include:

- **Convenience**: No need to commute to a therapist's office.
- **Scheduling Flexibility**: You might find session times outside standard office hours.
- **Broader Choice**: If you live in an area without many therapy options, online services can connect you with professionals anywhere in your region (subject to licensing rules).

Be sure any online platform you use is reputable and secure. Check that the therapist is licensed in your state or country. Sometimes insurance will cover online therapy, but it varies by plan.

Therapy Pitfalls to Avoid

1. **Unrealistic Expectations**: Therapy is not an instant fix. You may see small improvements over weeks or months.
2. **Lack of Follow-Through**: If a therapist suggests daily journaling or a time management exercise, skipping homework makes progress slower.

3. **Not Communicating**: If you feel a therapy method is not working or you are uncomfortable with an approach, speak up. Therapists are there to adjust and find what suits you.
4. **Stopping Too Soon**: Some men quit therapy as soon as they see small improvements. While it is good to celebrate progress, consider staying until you have a stable set of skills to maintain it.
5. **Avoiding Deeper Issues**: If emotional wounds or relationship conflicts are present, ignoring them limits therapy's success. Even if the main goal is handling ADHD, deeper issues can derail progress.

Blending Therapy with Other Approaches

- **Medication Plus Therapy**: Many men use both at the same time. Medication helps clear away the noise, while therapy teaches habits and coping skills.
- **Exercise and Nutrition**: Physical activity can boost mood and attention, complementing therapy. Good nutrition, such as protein-rich meals, can support stable energy levels.
- **Stress Management**: Techniques like breathing exercises or taking short nature walks can cut stress. High stress can worsen ADHD signs and hinder therapy efforts.
- **Support from Family/Friends**: If loved ones know you are in therapy, they can encourage you to keep your sessions and do homework. A spouse or close friend can also provide feedback on changes they see in your behavior.

Signs You Are Making Progress

It can be tough to measure therapy success, especially if changes happen gradually. Some markers of progress include:

- You find it easier to complete tasks you used to avoid or delay.
- Your anger flare-ups are less intense or less frequent.
- You catch yourself before interrupting others more often.
- You stick to a planning system for a month or two without abandoning it.

- You have a better sense of control in your day-to-day life, even if everything is not perfect.

Remember that progress can come in waves. You might have a few good weeks, then a setback. This is normal. Therapy is about long-term improvement, not quick perfection.

Cultural Views on Therapy

Different cultures have different attitudes about therapy. Some see it as normal, while others see it as a sign of weakness. If you come from a background where talking about personal struggles is frowned upon, therapy might feel uncomfortable at first. Keep in mind that ADHD is a valid condition, and seeking help is a practical step. A private, one-on-one setting can help you share your concerns without fear of judgment.

Planning for Future Challenges

Even after therapy ends, life will throw new tasks at you—maybe a new job, a change in family dynamics, or moving to a new place. Having learned therapy skills, you can apply them to new situations. You might do short "refresher" sessions with your therapist if you feel old patterns returning. Think of therapy as building a toolbox of methods that you can use for years to come.

Chapter 8: Social Life and Romantic Relationships

Introduction

ADHD does not just affect focus at work or study habits. It also plays a role in social interactions and close relationships. Men with ADHD can face misunderstandings, conflicts, or missed connections if they do not manage their challenges effectively. This chapter covers social life, dating, marriage, and how to handle the emotional issues that pop up in these areas.

While some men find it easy to make friends or start romantic connections, they may struggle to keep those bonds strong. Impulsivity or poor time management might lead to broken promises or sudden outbursts. On the other hand, some men feel shy or avoid social events because they fear embarrassing themselves. Understanding how ADHD intersects with social and romantic life can help you form meaningful connections and reduce conflicts.

Common Social Difficulties for Men with ADHD

1. **Interrupting Conversations**: When an idea strikes, a man with ADHD may blurt it out immediately. This can come across as disrespectful, even if not intended that way.
2. **Forgetting Important Social Details**: Birthdays, planned outings, or casual promises to friends can slip the mind, causing feelings of neglect or frustration in others.
3. **Shifting Interests**: Some men with ADHD develop strong enthusiasm for a new hobby or group, then lose interest quickly. This can confuse friends who are left wondering why you disappeared.
4. **Over-Talking or Zoning Out**: Men with ADHD might dominate a conversation about a favorite topic, then drift off when others

speak. This signals to friends that you only care about your own interests.
5. **Emotional Overreactions**: Social conflicts can trigger quick anger or defensiveness, especially if a man feels misunderstood.

These struggles do not mean you cannot have close, supportive friendships. It just requires awareness and strategies to keep interactions balanced.

Building and Keeping Friendships

1. Consistency and Reliability

Friends often value reliability. For men with ADHD, setting reminders about social events, using phone alarms for planned calls, or scheduling coffee meets on a digital calendar can show you care enough to remember. If you do forget or need to cancel, try to let the person know as early as possible and suggest a new time.

2. Active Listening

Practice turning your full attention toward the other person. Maintain eye contact, nod or give small verbal cues, and avoid checking your phone. If your mind starts to wander, bring it back by silently repeating key points they mention. After they finish, briefly restate what you heard to confirm you understand.

3. Avoid Impulsive Speeches

When you feel an urgent need to jump into the conversation, try to wait a few seconds. Ask yourself: "Is now the right moment to speak?" That brief pause can keep you from cutting someone off mid-sentence or hijacking the talk.

4. Honesty About ADHD

If you feel comfortable, sharing that you have ADHD can help friends understand why you sometimes lose track. This is optional, of course. But letting trusted friends know might reduce misunderstandings if you occasionally forget things or appear restless.

5. Balancing Communication

If you catch yourself talking a lot about your interests, ask the other person questions about theirs. Practicing a back-and-forth style can make them feel valued. This simple step can prevent the conversation from turning into a one-sided lecture.

Romantic Relationships: Common Pitfalls

1. **Uneven Distribution of Tasks**: If you share a home with a partner, they might feel they do most of the household chores. You might start a chore, get distracted, and never return. This can lead to resentment over time.
2. **Forgetting Special Occasions**: Anniversaries, a partner's big work presentation, or even smaller things like picking up groceries can slip from your mind. The partner might interpret it as a lack of care.
3. **Emotional Tension**: Impulsivity can lead to harsh words during arguments. Also, if you hyperfocus on a new interest, your partner might feel ignored.
4. **Financial Strains**: If ADHD leads to impulsive spending or missed bills, it can bring major stress into a relationship.
5. **Communication Breakdowns**: Quick boredom may cause you to tune out when your partner is discussing serious issues, making them feel unheard.

Strategies for Success in Romantic Relationships

1. Shared Calendar System

Use a shared digital calendar or a large wall calendar where you and your partner write down all events, appointments, and reminders. This reduces the chance of double-booking or forgetting important dates. Syncing phone calendars can help both of you see updates in real time.

2. Divide Tasks Based on Strengths

If you hate sorting mail but are good at cooking, perhaps you handle meal prep while your partner deals with incoming bills. By matching tasks to personal strengths, you both have a better chance of keeping routines stable and feeling less resentment.

3. Scheduled Talks

Pick a time each week—maybe Sunday evening—to discuss the coming week's plans and any concerns. This reduces the chance that serious talks are rushed or forgotten. Writing down main points ensures both remember what was decided.

4. Use Reminders and Alarms

If your partner needs you to buy groceries or pick up a child from practice, set alarms on your phone with labels. Even if you think you will remember, ADHD can play tricks. Alarms provide a backup.

5. Manage Your Emotions

If arguments get heated, step away for a brief period if you can. Calm your mind with a few deep breaths, then return to the conversation more level-headed. Emotional regulation is often a challenge with ADHD, but it can be improved by practicing simple calming tactics.

Dating with ADHD

Single men might wonder how ADHD affects dating. Common issues include planning dates (which requires organization), remembering small details about the person you are seeing, and being fully present during conversations.

- **Choose Active Dates**: If you tend to fidget or get bored, consider dates that involve movement or hands-on activities—like a short hike, bowling, or a fun cooking class. This keeps your mind engaged and can reduce nervous restlessness.
- **Listen and Ask Questions**: Show genuine curiosity about the other person's life. This helps avoid talking too much about yourself.
- **Be Realistic**: If planning is hard, do not overcomplicate the first date. A simpler plan you can follow through on is better than an elaborate idea you might forget or mess up.
- **Reflect After Each Date**: Jot down notes on what you enjoyed, details you learned about the person, and any potential next steps. This can prevent forgetting important information and help you plan future dates.

Long-Distance or Online Relationships

Men with ADHD may find some benefits in online or long-distance dating, such as more time to think before replying to a message. However, it can also be easy to lose track of scheduled video calls or forget to message back promptly. Setting specific times to talk can help keep the communication steady. Using apps that send alerts for upcoming calls is another way to stay consistent.

Dealing with Conflict

Conflict is normal in any relationship, but ADHD can intensify misunderstandings. If your partner or friend does not see how your attention slips or impulsivity feels uncontrollable, they may assume you do not care. Clear, calm explanations help:

- **Own Your Mistakes**: If you forgot an appointment, say, "I'm sorry. It slipped my mind. It's not that I don't care about you." Then discuss ways to prevent it next time, like setting a phone alert.
- **Avoid Escalation**: If voices start rising, suggest a short pause. Return once everyone has cooled down. Impulsive anger often leads to saying hurtful things that you regret.
- **Seek Outside Help**: Couples therapy or counseling can offer strategies unique to your situation. A neutral third party can ease tension and help each person see the other's viewpoint.

Social Anxiety and ADHD

Some men with ADHD also face social anxiety—worry about embarrassing themselves or being judged. This can cause them to avoid social settings or keep interactions shallow. If this sounds familiar:

- **Start Small**: Practice social skills with someone you trust, like a family member or one friend, before trying larger gatherings.
- **Prepare Topics**: If parties make you nervous, think of a few safe conversation topics (current events, sports, etc.). This reduces the panic of "What do I say now?"
- **Bring a Buddy**: Attending events with a supportive friend can provide a buffer and help you feel less isolated.
- **Consider Therapy**: A combination of therapy approaches (such as CBT) and ADHD management techniques can lessen anxiety.

Balancing Social Life and Personal Space

Men with ADHD may alternate between craving stimulation and feeling overwhelmed. You might love going out with friends but quickly get overloaded by noise or long conversations. Or you might find that you need frequent breaks to recharge. Communicating this need to friends or a partner is important:

- **Set Boundaries**: If you need downtime after work, let people know you will join them an hour later so you can decompress.

- **Plan Structured Hangouts**: Instead of loose, open-ended gatherings, propose activities with a clear end time (like seeing a movie or attending a fitness class). This gives you an exit point.
- **Use Safe Words**: If you have a partner who knows your triggers, consider a private signal to indicate you need to step away and regroup if you start feeling overwhelmed at a social event.

Technology and Social Connections

Social media and texting can help men with ADHD stay in touch, but they can also create distractions. Some pointers:

- **Use It as a Tool**: Group chats or event invites can keep you updated on friend gatherings. But avoid endless scrolling during a meet-up—your friends need your real attention.
- **Set Notification Limits**: Turning off notifications for non-essential apps can help you stay present in real-life conversations.
- **Schedule Online Catch-Ups**: If you have friends far away, plan a video call rather than relying on random messages. Structured calls reduce the chance of forgetting.

Family Gatherings and Obligations

Big family events (like holidays or reunions) can be overwhelming. Extended family might not understand ADHD, and you might be expected to socialize for hours. Strategies include:

- **Plan Ahead**: Ask about the schedule and who will attend. Knowing what to expect can reduce surprise stress.
- **Share Tasks**: If you are hosting, delegate tasks you struggle with (like decorating or remembering everyone's dietary needs). Focus on what you can handle well.
- **Take Quiet Breaks**: If the group is large, politely step outside or to another room for a few minutes to gather your thoughts.
- **Show Effort**: Even a small gesture—like giving your aunt a quick call to confirm the time or bringing a simple dish—can show you are trying. Family members often respond well to visible effort.

Social Skills Workshops

Some communities offer social skills training, either in-person or online. While these might feel more common for children and teens, adult-focused workshops do exist. They can teach techniques like reading body language, taking turns in conversation, or handling rejection gracefully. If this feels too formal, consider joining hobbies or interest-based clubs where you can practice these skills in a more natural setting.

Staying Motivated in Your Relationships

When life gets busy or ADHD feels like it is constantly in the way, it can be easy to neglect social bonds. But friendships and romantic ties add richness to life. Some tips to keep you motivated:

- **Set Social Goals**: Maybe aim to meet up with one friend each week or send a check-in text to someone you value.
- **Review the Positives**: After a good time with friends or a sweet date, jot down what made it enjoyable. This serves as a reminder to keep social connections going.
- **Celebrate Small Wins** (Use another word if needed): Did you remember a friend's birthday this time? Recognize that as progress. Did you avoid interrupting your partner during a serious talk? That is another sign of growth.
- **Ask for Feedback**: Trusted friends or your partner can gently tell you if certain ADHD behaviors are affecting your interactions. This insight can guide you on what to work on next.

Handling Breakups or Social Letdowns

Rejection or loss of friendships can be extra tough when you already struggle with self-esteem or emotional regulation. If a romantic relationship ends or a friend pulls away:

- **Self-Reflection**: Honestly review if ADHD-related behaviors contributed to the split. Do not beat yourself up, but note patterns for future improvement.

- **Seek Support**: Talk to a counselor or trusted friends. Bottling up emotions can intensify negative thoughts.
- **Accept Responsibility When Needed**: If you made mistakes—like forgetting constant promises—own up. Apologize if that is still possible.
- **Look Forward**: It helps to use what you learned to improve future relationships. Everyone makes mistakes, and ADHD often just amplifies them. Growth is possible with consistent effort.

Conclusion of Chapter 8

Social life and romantic relationships can be greatly affected by ADHD, but this does not mean men with ADHD are doomed to lonely or chaotic connections. By learning practical skills—like using shared calendars, practicing active listening, and managing impulses—you can build stronger friendships and healthier romantic bonds. Openness about your condition (where appropriate) can also help people around you see that you are not careless; you are dealing with a real attention issue.

Relationships are a two-way street, so communication, planning, and empathy go a long way. Whether it is a friend, a new date, or a long-term partner, showing you are willing to try solutions (like phone reminders or weekly check-ins) can help keep things running smoothly. Even if missteps happen—as they often do with ADHD—the willingness to acknowledge them and seek better habits shows growth. Over time, consistent effort can transform misunderstandings into supportive, meaningful ties that enrich your life.

Chapter 9: Career Challenges and Workplace Tips

Introduction

Many men with ADHD can excel in the working world if they find the right environment, understand their needs, and put helpful supports in place. Yet, the day-to-day demands of a job—such as managing time, meeting deadlines, and dealing with coworkers—can be a big challenge when ADHD signs are at play. Some men get stuck in low-paying jobs or constantly switch employers because they struggle to keep up with tasks. Others might do well for a while but then lose steam once the initial excitement wears off.

This chapter looks at the common hurdles men with ADHD face in careers, how to handle them, and ways to make the most of personal strengths. It does not matter if you are just starting your work life or if you have been employed for years and feel stuck. By learning tips and methods, you can handle job demands more smoothly. It is important to note that there is no one-size-fits-all plan. Different people do better in different types of jobs or schedules. The ideas here are meant to guide you, and you can adjust them based on your own situation.

Common Workplace Struggles

1. **Time Management**: For men with ADHD, an hour can pass in what feels like a few minutes, especially if the task is not interesting. This leads to missed deadlines or rushed work.
2. **Disorganization**: Piles of papers, cluttered email inboxes, and lost documents are frequent problems that can create a bad impression.
3. **Procrastination**: Putting off tasks can be driven by boredom, fear of failure, or just lack of attention. This can result in a never-ending cycle of scrambling at the last minute.

4. **Impulsive Actions**: Speaking out in meetings without thinking, firing off emails too quickly, or making quick decisions without consulting others can cause friction.
5. **Restlessness**: Staying seated for a long time is tough for some men with ADHD. They may fidget, pace, or find reasons to move around, which can annoy coworkers if not managed.
6. **Boredom with Repetitive Tasks**: Most jobs have some repetitive or mundane parts. Losing focus during these tasks can lead to errors or incomplete work.

Understanding these struggles is the first step toward finding solutions. It might feel hopeless if you have faced these same issues at job after job, but there are practical ways to adjust your workspace and your methods so you can succeed.

Choosing the Right Job or Field

Not every job is a good match for ADHD-related traits. Some men might thrive in busy, fast-paced fields that offer variety—like emergency services, event planning, or sales—while others need quieter settings with fewer distractions to get things done. Factors to think about:

- **Level of Stimulation**: Do you perform better when the work is high-energy, or do you need a calm environment to focus?
- **Structure vs. Freedom**: Some people do well with strict rules and clear tasks, while others do better with creative freedom and new projects.
- **Hands-On Work vs. Desk Work**: If you need to move around, a job that involves physical activity or travel might be more suitable than sitting at a computer all day.
- **Teamwork vs. Solo Tasks**: Consider how you handle group settings. Do group dynamics keep you engaged, or do they create extra distractions?

Choosing a job that matches your strengths does not mean you avoid all challenges. Every workplace has routines and responsibilities that might feel dull. But if the bulk of the job lines up with your abilities, you will spend less time fighting against ADHD quirks and more time using your natural talents.

Organizing Your Workplace

1. Create Clear Zones

If you have a desk, label or split it into zones. For example, one area for incoming papers, another for completed tasks, and a space for personal items. This reduces the chance of shuffling everything into random piles.

2. Color-Coding and Labels

Using color-coded folders or labels can help you locate files quickly. For instance, use a red folder for urgent tasks, a blue folder for reference materials, and so forth. Label drawers or shelves so you do not waste time searching for things.

3. Keep Essential Items Within Reach

Put commonly used tools—like pens, sticky notes, phone chargers—within arm's reach. That way, you do not wander around the office looking for them, which often leads to distractions.

4. Digital Organization

On your computer, make clear folder structures and name files in a consistent way. Set up rules in your email program to sort messages into folders. Some men with ADHD find it helpful to keep their inbox nearly empty by archiving emails as soon as they handle them, so the main inbox only has pending tasks.

Time Management Tricks

1. The Timer Method

Break your work into blocks, such as 25 minutes of focused work followed by a 5-minute break. Setting a timer helps you stay on track. After 25 minutes, stand up, stretch, or get a drink of water. Then reset the timer. This not only fights boredom but also trains you to work in short, effective sprints.

2. Task Lists with Priorities

Writing everything you need to do in one big list can be overwhelming. Instead, pick the top three tasks for the day. These should be the ones that truly matter. Finish those first before moving on to smaller items. This way, you ensure important tasks do not fall through the cracks.

3. Schedule Tasks in Your Calendar

Instead of a simple to-do list, put tasks directly into your calendar with start and end times. For example:

- 9:00–9:30 AM: Answer emails
- 9:30–10:30 AM: Work on Project X
- 10:30–10:45 AM: Break

Treat these entries like actual appointments. It helps keep your day structured and reduces the urge to get sidetracked.

4. "One-Page Rule"

Some men with ADHD write overly long notes or have dozens of sticky papers on their desk. If you struggle with too much clutter, try keeping a single piece of paper or a small notebook where you jot down the top items for the day. Update it daily. This forces you to focus on the essentials.

Handling Procrastination

1. Start with the Easiest Part

If you have a large project, begin with the simplest piece to gain momentum. Feeling that small success can reduce the mental block around tackling the harder parts.

2. Reward Yourself

Set a mini-reward for completing a dreaded task—maybe a short walk, a snack, or checking social media briefly. Knowing a small treat is waiting can push you to start.

3. Public Accountability

Tell a coworker or supervisor about your deadline, or put a note on your office wall saying, "Finish X by 2 PM." When others know about your commitment, it can add a sense of responsibility that fights the urge to postpone work.

4. Use Visual Progress Tools

For ongoing projects, keep a simple progress chart on your wall or desktop. Mark off each step completed. Seeing your progress inch forward can spark more effort.

Managing Impulsivity at Work

1. Pause Before Responding

If you tend to blurt out answers in meetings, practice waiting a couple of seconds after someone finishes speaking. Take a breath, think about your response, then speak. This small pause can save you from interrupting or making comments you regret.

2. Draft Emails Before Sending

Impulsive emailing can lead to misunderstandings. Type your message in a separate document. Read it over for tone and correctness. Then, once you are sure, copy and paste it into the actual email and send. This extra step helps prevent hasty communication.

3. Avoid Quick Decisions on Major Issues

If your job involves choices with big consequences—like budgets or project directions—try to buy time before committing. Say something like, "Let me think on this for a moment," or "I'd like to review the details before we finalize." This gives your mind space to consider.

4. Limit Chat Distractions

If you find yourself impulsively chatting with coworkers, set boundaries. Maybe only chat when you are on a break or during lunch. If your environment allows, use headphones to signal you need focus time.

Dealing with Coworkers and Supervisors

1. Be Open if Appropriate

You do not have to disclose your ADHD to everyone. But if you have a supportive supervisor, telling them you have attention challenges might allow for small changes that make a big difference—like a quieter workspace or flexible break times. Only share if you feel it is safe and beneficial.

2. Ask for Clarity

If instructions are vague or tasks feel confusing, speak up. It is better to clarify your role than to get it wrong because you were unsure. Some men with ADHD hesitate to ask questions, fearing they look bad. In reality, seeking clarity often shows you care about doing a good job.

3. Control Emotional Reactions

If a coworker criticizes your work or you clash over a task, pause before replying. Men with ADHD can sometimes have quick bursts of anger. Take a short walk or sip water. Return to the conversation with a calmer tone.

4. Practice Good Listening Skills

Repeat back what the other person says in your own words to confirm you heard it right. For example, "So you want the report done by Tuesday at noon, correct?" This helps avoid misunderstandings and shows respect.

Movement and Breaks

Men with ADHD often feel restless when seated for too long. Short breaks can boost focus:

- **Stand or Stretch Often**: Even 30 seconds of standing or stretching can help if you feel jittery.
- **Use Walking Meetings**: If your workplace allows it, suggest a short walk while discussing ideas with a coworker. This keeps your body active and your mind engaged.
- **Fidget Tools**: Some workplaces are open to small stress balls or fidget gadgets. If it does not distract others, these can channel restless energy without forcing you to leave your desk.

Handling Long Meetings

Meetings can be a nightmare if they drag on. Some tips:

- **Take Notes**: This keeps your hands busy and your mind on the topic. Summaries of the main points help you recall details later.
- **Ask Questions**: This can keep you engaged, but do not overdo it. Make sure the question is relevant.
- **Request an Agenda**: If you know the meeting outline in advance, you can prepare yourself for the topics and track your attention more easily.

Job Transitions and Changes

If you frequently switch jobs, it might be due to boredom or unresolved ADHD challenges. While changing jobs can sometimes be helpful, try to address the core issues as well:

- **Reflection**: Note which tasks caused problems in past jobs. Were they related to organization, communication, or something else?
- **Skill Building**: If you plan to move into a new role, consider improving your executive function skills—like time management—so you do not bring the same problems with you.
- **Explore Accommodations**: Some workplaces have official policies to support employees with attention difficulties—like flexible schedules or quiet work areas.

Remote Work Considerations

Remote or hybrid work can be great if you can set up a low-distraction environment at home. But it can also lead to problems if you struggle with self-discipline:

- **Designated Workspace**: Avoid working in your living room or bedroom if possible. Having a separate spot can help you stay in "work mode."
- **Structured Schedule**: Even though you are at home, keep clear work hours. Plan breaks and commit to finishing tasks on time.
- **Use Accountability**: Check in with your team or boss once or twice a day. Knowing you have to show progress can keep you on track.
- **Limit Personal Distractions**: If you are tempted by TV, games, or household chores, set rules—like no TV until after your main tasks are done.

Building on Strengths

Many men with ADHD bring unique strengths to the workplace:

- **Creativity**: The ADHD mind often jumps between ideas quickly, sparking new solutions others might miss.
- **Energy and Enthusiasm**: When you are interested in a project, you might dive into it with a lot of drive, inspiring coworkers.
- **Ability to Handle Crises**: ADHD brains can thrive under pressure. Tight deadlines or dynamic problems may keep you fully engaged.
- **Good People Skills**: Some men with ADHD are highly social and can make strong connections with clients or colleagues, boosting teamwork.

Recognizing these strong points can help you pick a career path that highlights them. While you work on improving organization, you can still make the most of your positive traits.

Stress Management at Work

Stress can worsen ADHD signs, causing more forgetfulness or impulsivity:

- **Short Relaxation Methods**: Practice simple breathing exercises. Inhale for a count of four, hold for four, exhale for four. Repeat a few times. This calms your mind and body.
- **Plan Buffer Time**: If you have a meeting at 3:00 PM, aim to finish your prior task by 2:50 PM, giving yourself time to transition. This lowers the feeling of constant rush.
- **Stay Hydrated and Fed**: Low blood sugar or dehydration can affect focus. Keep water and healthy snacks around.
- **Get Support**: If stress levels are too high, consider talking with a therapist, coach, or employee assistance program if your company offers one.

Knowing When to Seek Help

If your ADHD signs are causing major work problems—like repeated write-ups, frequent job losses, or severe stress—it may be time to seek outside help:

- **Professional Counseling or Coaching**: A counselor specializing in ADHD can teach strategies for on-the-job challenges. A coach can hold you accountable for daily or weekly goals.
- **Medical Check**: If you suspect your medication or health issues are affecting job performance, consult a doctor. A medication adjustment might make a big difference.
- **HR or Union Resources**: In some workplaces, talking to HR (Human Resources) or a union representative about possible accommodations can open doors to helpful support. Just make sure to approach it in a way that feels safe and aligns with workplace policies.

Conclusion of Chapter 9

Men with ADHD face real struggles in managing tasks, time, and interactions at work. However, these challenges do not need to stand in the way of a fulfilling career. Through organization techniques, mindful planning, and better communication skills, you can keep distractions under control and thrive in your role. It helps to pick a job environment that aligns with your strengths and to use tools like timers, color-coding, and structured schedules.

Even in less-than-ideal work conditions, small shifts—like using a single to-do list and scheduling short breaks—can yield big benefits over time. If extra help is needed, do not hesitate to seek professional advice or coaching. By understanding how ADHD affects your work life and putting solid strategies in place, you can turn career hurdles into manageable tasks and find success on your own terms.

Chapter 10: Education, Study Methods, and Memory Tricks

Introduction

Men with ADHD often find formal education or training programs challenging. Whether you are in college, attending a trade school, or taking work-related courses, the demands on focus, organization, and memory can be high. Some men who coasted through school as kids find adult education harder because of larger reading loads, deadlines, and less direct supervision. Others might be returning to study after years of working, feeling out of practice with textbooks and assignments.

This chapter provides strategies to help men with ADHD do better in educational settings. It covers managing time, reducing distractions, taking effective notes, and boosting memory. Many of these tips also apply to on-the-job training or self-guided online courses. With the right methods, you can improve your learning process and reduce the stress that so often accompanies school tasks.

Choosing the Right Program or Course

1. **Mode of Delivery**: Some men do better with in-person classes where they can ask questions and see the instructor face to face. Others might prefer online courses that let them work at their own pace.
2. **Schedule**: If you struggle to wake up early, an 8 AM class might be a disaster. Look for timeslots that align with your energy levels.
3. **Subject Interest**: ADHD brains often lock onto interesting topics more easily. If possible, select courses that spark your curiosity.
4. **Class Size and Support**: Smaller classes can give you more direct help from the teacher. Also check if the school offers tutoring or disability support services.

Picking a learning environment that aligns with your strengths can reduce the amount of sheer willpower needed to stay focused. Even so, some boring or required classes will always be part of the deal, so having strategies to tackle them is crucial.

Setting Up a Study Space

1. Minimize Distractions

Your study area should be free of clutter and loud noises. If you live with others, try to find a quiet corner or time when the home is calmer. Noise-canceling headphones or gentle background music can help block out random sounds.

2. Ergonomic Comfort

Choose a chair and desk that fit your height so you do not get back or neck pain. A comfortable setup can help you stay seated longer without fidgeting or discomfort.

3. Keep Supplies Handy

Have pens, highlighters, note cards, or whatever tools you need within reach so you do not keep getting up to look for things. Each interruption is a chance for your mind to wander off.

4. Digital Tools

If you study on a computer, consider browser extensions that block distracting websites for a set time. Keep only necessary tabs open. If you need to watch videos for class, resist the urge to click unrelated content.

Time Management for Studies

1. Break Down Assignments

If you have a 10-page paper, do not try to write it all at once. Split the project into smaller steps—choose a topic, find sources, draft an outline, write a rough draft, revise. Schedule each step on different days or timeslots.

2. Use a Planner or Calendar

Write all due dates as soon as you get your course syllabus. Then, plan backward from the deadlines. If a paper is due in three weeks, schedule each stage of that paper so you are not rushing the night before.

3. Short Study Blocks with Breaks

The same approach that works at work—timers—also helps with studying. Study for 25 minutes, take a 5-minute break, and repeat. After a few cycles, take a longer break. This method keeps you fresh and helps you focus better during each short block.

4. Avoid Marathon Sessions

Men with ADHD often find it impossible to concentrate for hours straight. Spreading study sessions across days is more effective than cramming all at once. Cramming also increases stress, which can worsen focus problems.

Note-Taking Methods

1. Active Listening or Reading

Instead of copying everything verbatim, focus on identifying main points. Ask yourself, "What is the key idea here? How does it link to what I already know?" This approach keeps your brain engaged.

2. Using Headings and Bullet Points

Structuring notes with clear headings, subheadings, and bullet points helps you quickly scan for information later. It also forces you to organize concepts as you write.

3. Visual Aids

Some men with ADHD are visual learners. Sketching simple diagrams, flowcharts, or mind maps can help you remember how ideas connect. These graphics do not have to be pretty; they just need to reflect the concepts in a visual way.

4. Color-Coding

You can color-code your notes by topic or importance. For instance, use red for main ideas, blue for supporting details, and green for examples. This helps your mind see patterns in the text.

Memory-Boosting Tricks

1. Chunking

Our brains remember information better in small groups rather than long strings. Group facts into categories or break big ideas into shorter parts. For example, if you are memorizing historical dates, group them by century or by key events.

2. Repetition

Repetition strengthens memory. Review your notes soon after a class to lock them into your mind. Then do quick refreshers every few days. This "spacing" method of repeating material over time is more effective than a single mass review.

3. Teach Someone Else

Explain a concept to a friend or family member. Teaching forces you to put ideas into your own words and identify any gaps in your understanding. It also helps store the information more solidly in your memory.

4. Mnemonics

Use acronyms, short phrases, or mental images to remember details. For instance, to recall a series of items, create a funny sentence where each word starts with the same letter as the items in the list. Silly images or stories often stick in the mind better than plain text.

Handling Reading Assignments

1. Preview the Text

Skim headings, subheadings, and any bold or italic text before reading. Look at summaries or chapter outlines if available. This gives your brain a roadmap and helps you focus on key areas.

2. Active Reading

Highlight or underline main points, but do not go overboard and highlight everything. Write short notes in the margins, such as "Key term" or "Compare to page 43." This keeps your mind from drifting.

3. Summarize After Each Section

Pause after reading a chunk of text. Ask yourself, "What did I just learn?" Write a quick summary in your own words. If you cannot summarize, you might need to reread that part.

4. Use Audiobooks or Text-to-Speech

If your course material is available in audio format or you can convert text to speech, listen to it while following along in the text. Hearing and seeing the words at the same time can help you absorb the material better.

Group Studies and Peer Support

1. Finding the Right Study Buddy

Pick someone who is serious about the work and does not distract you with constant side conversations. Make sure you both agree on how to spend study time.

2. Structured Sessions

Plan a clear goal for each group study meeting—such as reviewing a chapter or solving a set of problems. This prevents the session from turning into random chatting.

3. Explaining Concepts to Each Other

Take turns teaching a topic. This can highlight areas one person understands better and helps the other catch up. It also keeps everyone engaged.

4. Be Honest About Distractors

If you notice you or your buddy are going off-topic too often, call it out gently. Agree on ways to get back on track, like setting a quick timer for focus.

Dealing with Tests and Exams

1. Early Preparation

Men with ADHD who cram at the last minute often panic because they cannot handle hours of forced concentration. Start reviewing days or weeks in advance, in small doses.

2. Practice With Sample Questions

Doing practice tests or sample questions is one of the best ways to prepare. It helps you recognize what types of questions might appear and test your recall under realistic conditions.

3. Plan Your Time in the Exam

If the test is timed, scan the questions quickly, note the ones you can answer easily, and tackle them first. Mark harder ones for later so you do not get stuck on one question too long.

4. Double-Check for Small Errors

Take a quick pass over your answers if time allows. Men with ADHD can miss small details, so verifying can catch silly mistakes. Keep an eye on the clock so you do not overdo the review and miss finishing.

Online Classes and E-Learning

1. Set a Routine

Online courses often have flexible schedules, which can be both good and bad. If you do not set strict times to watch lectures or do assignments, you might fall behind. Block out specific study times in your calendar.

2. Interact in Discussion Boards

Posting questions or responding to classmates can keep you engaged. Participation also forces you to pay attention to course material so you can contribute meaningfully.

3. Minimize Digital Distractions

Close all unrelated tabs and apps. If needed, use website blockers. It is easy to lose hours browsing the web when you should be studying.

4. Stay in Touch with Instructors

If you struggle with concepts or time management, email your instructor or teaching assistant for help. Many are willing to clarify points or provide extra resources.

Handling Anxiety and Pressure

Exams and deadlines can amplify anxiety in men with ADHD:

- **Practice Relaxation**: Before studying or an exam, try slow breathing or simple stretches to calm your nerves.
- **Ask About Accommodations**: Some schools allow extended test time or a quiet room if you have documentation of ADHD. This can remove some pressure.
- **Talk to a Counselor**: If the stress is overwhelming, a counselor can teach coping methods or adjust your study plan.
- **Avoid Excessive Caffeine**: High caffeine can make anxiety worse and cause jitters that disrupt concentration.

Balancing School with Other Responsibilities

If you are juggling a job, family, or other duties along with classes, planning becomes even more important:

- **Make a Master Schedule**: Include work shifts, class times, study blocks, and family activities in one calendar to see any conflicts.
- **Prioritize Tasks**: Decide which responsibilities are non-negotiable (like work deadlines) and which can be flexible.
- **Communicate with Others**: Let family or roommates know your study times so they can avoid disturbing you. See if coworkers can adjust schedules if you have critical school deadlines.
- **Avoid Overcommitment**: Taking on too many classes or hours at work can lead to burnout. It is often better to do fewer tasks well than to overload yourself and risk failing or dropping out.

Support from Disability Services

Many colleges and trade schools have an office for disability services. They can offer:

- **Extra Test Time or Private Rooms**
- **Note-Takers or Recording Lectures**
- **Course Materials in Alternate Formats**
- **One-on-One Meetings for Strategy Building**

You usually need documentation of ADHD, but once registered, you can tap into these supports. It can feel awkward to ask for help, but remember these services exist for a reason. They can be the difference between struggling alone and performing at your best.

Staying Motivated

1. Connect Lessons to Real-Life Goals

Ask yourself how this course or skill helps you in your career or personal interests. Linking learning to a real goal can boost motivation when coursework feels dull.

2. Track Your Wins

Keep a small log of completed assignments or good test scores. Seeing evidence of progress can encourage you to push further.

3. Build Rest into Your Schedule

Constant studying without breaks leads to burnout. Plan leisure activities or simple pleasures. Just be careful not to let them become procrastination traps.

4. Find Mentors or Role Models

If you know someone who succeeded in the same field, talk to them. Ask about their study tips or how they overcame setbacks. Their guidance can inspire you and give you fresh ideas.

Avoiding Burnout

Burnout happens when stress and workload become too heavy for too long:

- **Watch for Warning Signs**: Extreme tiredness, dropping grades, missing deadlines, or feeling hopeless can signal burnout.
- **Evaluate Your Workload**: Maybe you need to drop a class, switch to part-time, or lighten your course load.
- **Self-Care**: Get enough sleep, eat well, and allow time for hobbies or social life. This balance is crucial for ADHD brains that can get stuck in hyperfocus or total avoidance.
- **Seek Professional Help**: If burnout is deep, a counselor or coach can help reorganize your approach and find fresh ways to cope.

Chapter 11: Money Management and Budget Tips

Introduction

Finances can be a tricky area for men with ADHD. Many day-to-day money tasks—such as keeping receipts, remembering due dates, and tracking spending—require organization and attention to detail. When bills pile up or bank balances dip, stress can build, making ADHD signs worse. Some men may buy items on impulse and regret it later, while others may struggle with scattered bills that never get paid on time.

Still, it is important to know that managing money well is possible. It requires practical systems and some discipline, but you do not need to be perfect at everything. By setting up structures that work for the ADHD mind, you can reduce financial mistakes, avoid debt spirals, and even save for future goals. This chapter will explore common money hurdles for men with ADHD and offer tips on budgeting, paying bills, tracking spending, and building healthy financial habits that can last.

Why ADHD Makes Money Management Hard

1. Poor Time Awareness

Men with ADHD can have trouble sensing time. A bill that is due in two weeks might feel like it is "ages away." Then, it sneaks up and becomes overdue. Without a clear system for tracking deadlines, these surprises can lead to late fees or even utility cutoffs.

2. Impulse Spending

The ADHD brain often seeks novelty or quick excitement. An unexpected sale, a tempting gadget, or a fun activity can trigger a sudden urge to buy.

Without thinking ahead, you might swipe your card or click "purchase" online. Later, you could regret the expense.

3. Disorganized Paperwork

Receipts, statements, and letters from the bank can pile up if there is no routine for sorting them. You might find them in random drawers or on your car seat. When it comes time to track your spending or file taxes, you do not have the documents you need.

4. Boredom with Administrative Tasks

Budgeting and record-keeping can seem dull. Men with ADHD may find these tasks extra unpleasant, leading to procrastination. When you do get started, you might get overwhelmed by the details.

5. Difficulty Planning for the Future

Some people with ADHD focus on the present moment more than the long term. Saving for retirement or creating a plan for major purchases can feel irrelevant until it is too late. This can cause problems later on, when big expenses appear and you are not prepared.

First Steps: Knowing Your Financial Picture

Gather All Data

Before any improvement can happen, you need a clear look at your current money situation. This means:

- Listing your monthly income (including wages, side gigs, or help from family).
- Listing all fixed expenses (rent, car payments, insurance, phone bill).
- Estimating variable expenses (food, gas, personal items).
- Checking credit card balances and any loans.

This process can be boring, but it is a must. If you find it too daunting, break it down into tasks. For example, on Monday, collect your bills. On Tuesday, review your bank statements. On Wednesday, look at your credit card statements. Slowly piece the puzzle together. It is normal to feel discouraged at first if the numbers are not great. But facing them is the first step to making changes.

Organize Important Documents

Men with ADHD often benefit from a simple, labeled filing system. You can use either physical folders or digital ones. For physical documents, create folders with clear labels such as "Bills to Pay," "Paid Bills," "Bank Statements," "Tax Documents," and "Receipts." If you prefer digital, scan or download statements and keep them in labeled folders on your computer (for example, "2025 Bank Statements" or "2025 Bills").

A single messy pile of papers is a recipe for missing due dates. Knowing exactly where to put each document as soon as you get it can reduce the chaos. Take 5 minutes each day or each week—whatever suits you—to file any new papers or emails.

Setting a Budget

Keep It Simple

Some budgeting methods are very detailed, requiring multiple categories and daily tracking. This can overwhelm men with ADHD. Try a simpler approach first. You might use a basic spreadsheet with columns for income, fixed expenses, and variable expenses. Or you could use an envelope system, where you set aside cash in labeled envelopes (like "Food," "Gas," "Entertainment"). When the envelope is empty, you know you have hit that month's limit for that category.

Give Every Dollar a Job

One popular system says you should "give every dollar a job." This means you decide in advance what you will do with each bit of income. For example, if you earn $3,000 a month, you might assign $1,000 to rent, $300 to groceries, $200 to utilities, $300 to debt payments, $300 to savings, $100 to fun, and so on until every dollar is "used." The goal is to make your money serve specific purposes rather than just floating around until you spend it on impulses.

Automatic Transfers

Men with ADHD often do better if they remove the chance of forgetting. Automatic transfers can be a big help. You can set up your bank so that right after you get paid, a certain amount automatically moves into savings or toward a loan. This way, you never see the money in your main checking account. It reduces the temptation to spend and ensures you are meeting savings goals.

Apps and Tools

Plenty of budgeting apps exist that can link with your bank accounts, track spending automatically, and show you where your money goes. Examples include specialized budgeting apps or even the budgeting features of many bank websites. Explore the options to find one that feels intuitive. If an app is too complicated, you might abandon it. So pick one that is user-friendly and requires minimal effort.

Paying Bills on Time

Use Automatic Bill Pay

Most utility companies, credit card providers, and loan servicers allow you to set up automatic payments. This is a big relief for those who forget due dates. As long as you have enough money in your account, your bills get paid without you lifting a finger. Be careful to check your account balance to avoid overdrafts.

Calendar Reminders

If automatic payments are not an option or you prefer more control, set calendar reminders on your phone or computer. Input all bill due dates and have your device alert you a few days before. This way, you have time to move money around if needed. Consistent reminders remove the mental load of trying to recall every deadline.

Consolidate Bills if Possible

If you have multiple credit cards, consider merging balances onto one card with a favorable rate, if that is an option. The goal is to have fewer separate due dates. For some men with ADHD, fewer accounts mean fewer opportunities to slip up.

Weekly Money Check-Ins

Rather than ignoring your finances until the end of the month, do a quick weekly review. Look at your bank balance, see which bills have been paid, and confirm which ones are coming up. This routine keeps you aware of your money without it becoming a huge chore.

Dealing with Impulse Spending

Wait It Out

If you see something you want to buy, make a rule that you must wait 24 hours (or even 48 hours) before finalizing the purchase. Many times, the urge fades once you have had a chance to think it over. This simple delay can prevent a lot of regret.

Use Cash for Problem Areas

For categories where you often overspend—such as eating out or hobby items—think about using cash. Once you run out of the cash set aside for that category, you know you have hit your limit. Physical money can be more real and tangible than just swiping a card.

Unsubscribe from Temptations

Advertising emails and social media ads can trigger impulsive buys. If you find yourself constantly clicking "buy now," unsubscribe from store newsletters and turn off notifications from shopping apps. The fewer temptations in front of you, the better.

Accountability Partner

You might have a friend or family member you trust who can serve as a check on big purchases. If you want to buy something over a certain amount—let's say $100 or $200—agree to talk it through with that person first. Often, just having that conversation helps you see if the purchase is really necessary.

Saving for Future Goals

Start Small

Men with ADHD can find large goals—like saving thousands of dollars—overwhelming. Start with something modest, such as saving $20 a week or $50 a month. Automatic transfers, as mentioned, can help. Over time, small amounts grow, and you get used to the habit of saving.

Name Each Savings Goal

It can be more motivating to label savings accounts with names like "Car Fund," "Vacation," or "Emergency Fund" rather than just calling everything "Savings." These clear labels remind you of why you are putting money aside, which can reduce the urge to dip into it for random spending.

Create an Emergency Fund

Unexpected events—like car repairs or a sudden medical bill—can blow up your budget if you do not have spare cash. Building a small emergency fund, even $500 to $1,000 at first, can give peace of mind. This fund should be separate from your main checking account, so you are not tempted to use it for everyday wants.

Invest Wisely

If you have high-interest debt (like credit cards), it is often best to pay that off first before investing. However, if you have some spare funds, consider learning about simple, low-cost investments. Many men with ADHD do better with set-it-and-forget-it investments, such as index funds or retirement accounts that automatically invest your money. Once set up, these do not require daily attention, reducing the chance of impulsive decisions.

Debt Management

Face Your Debt

Like bills, debt can feel overwhelming, but ignoring it will only make things worse. Write down each debt, the balance, the interest rate, and the minimum monthly payment. This clarity, while uncomfortable, lets you pick a strategy to tackle it.

Snowball vs. Avalanche Methods

Two popular debt payment strategies:

- **Snowball**: Pay off the smallest debt first (while making minimum payments on the others). This gives a quick sense of progress. Then move on to the next smallest.
- **Avalanche**: Pay extra on the debt with the highest interest rate first. This saves more money in the long run.

Choose the one that you will stick to—some prefer the quick wins of the snowball method; others like the efficiency of the avalanche method.

Negotiate with Creditors

If you are struggling, consider calling credit card companies or lenders to see if they can lower your interest rate or work out a payment plan. Many creditors are open to helping customers who reach out proactively. This can reduce monthly payments or fees.

Seek Professional Help

For severe debt, a nonprofit credit counseling agency might help you create a budget or set up a debt management plan. They can sometimes negotiate on your behalf. But be cautious about for-profit debt settlement companies, as some might charge high fees or damage your credit further.

Technology and Tricks

Budgeting Apps

Various apps automatically categorize transactions from your bank account. This reduces the manual labor of writing down every expense. Examples include well-known budgeting services that connect securely to your accounts. Check your phone's app store for options with high ratings and read user feedback.

Bill Payment Alerts

Most banks and credit card apps let you set custom alerts, such as a text message when your balance drops below a certain amount, or when a bill is due soon. These can keep you on your toes without requiring constant manual checking.

Virtual Envelopes

Some modern banking platforms let you divide your checking account balance into "sub-accounts" or "spaces." You can label these spaces for rent, groceries, or fun money. This mimics the old envelope system but in a digital way.

Receipt Scanning

If you are the type who needs to track expenses for tax reasons or personal records, using a receipt scanning app can be a lifesaver. Simply snap a photo of the receipt, and the app logs the amount, date, and category. Then you do not have to keep a stack of physical receipts.

Money Mindset and Emotions

Address Shame or Guilt

Men with ADHD might feel ashamed of financial struggles, especially if they compare themselves to friends who seem more stable. Recognize that ADHD can play a big role in money issues, and it is not just lack of willpower. Accepting this can help you move forward without drowning in self-blame.

Build a Realistic Budget

Do not create a super strict budget that does not allow for any fun. That often leads to resentment or binges of spending. Allow yourself some personal spending money each month—even if it is small—so you do not feel deprived.

Positive Reinforcement

When you handle money well—like paying bills on time for a month—acknowledge that success. A small reward or a positive note on your calendar can motivate you to keep going. This approach mirrors some behavioral strategies, reinforcing the good habit.

Seek Support, Not Judgment

If you have a spouse or partner, work as a team instead of blaming each other for money issues. Also, share your wins and setbacks with a trusted friend or counselor if that helps. Sometimes, talking about money openly can reduce stress.

Unique Tips to Match ADHD Traits

Engaging Your Interest

Gamify your finances if that helps. Some apps use progress bars or fun visuals that can keep you more involved. Or, create personal challenges, like "No Restaurant Eating for 10 Days" and see if you can beat your own record.

Handling Boredom

If you find balancing accounts dull, pair it with something you enjoy, like listening to your favorite music or sipping a hot drink. Keep the finance session short, maybe 10 or 15 minutes, so you can tolerate it better.

Impulse Gap

Practice pausing at checkout. Even if you are standing in line with an item, tell yourself you will think about it for 30 seconds. Ask, "Do I really need this?" This mental gap can block the immediate rush to buy.

Using Physical Reminders

Stick a note on your wallet or computer screen with your main money goal ("Pay off credit card," "Save $500 for repairs"). Seeing that reminder can cut through an impulsive moment.

Planning for Bigger Life Events

Car Purchases

Cars can be expensive and often include monthly payments, insurance, and upkeep. Research models that fit your budget before visiting a dealer, and try not to let a flashy pitch lead you into a loan you cannot handle. Consider setting a firm maximum price or monthly payment and refusing to go above it.

Housing Decisions

Rent vs. buy is a personal choice, but men with ADHD must be aware that a house comes with many maintenance tasks and potential unexpected costs. Factor these in if you decide to buy. If you rent, consider what you can afford comfortably, given your income and other obligations.

Family Costs

If you have a spouse or kids, money planning becomes more complex. You might need to think about childcare, education expenses, and insurance. Having clear communication with your partner about bills, shared accounts, and future goals is crucial. Frequent check-ins help you both stay on track.

Retirement

Retirement might seem far off, but the earlier you start saving, the easier it is. Many jobs offer retirement accounts with employer matches. If yours does, contribute at least enough to get the full match. It is effectively free money. If not, look at opening an individual retirement account (IRA) or similar. Automate contributions so you do not have to think about it every month.

Reviewing and Tweaking the Plan

Your budget and strategies are not set in stone. Men with ADHD might need to adjust often. Maybe an app you liked at first no longer helps you, or your income changes. That is okay. Keep what works and change what does not.

Monthly Reflections

At the end of each month, take 10-15 minutes to see how you did. Did you overspend in certain areas? Did you pay all bills on time? Celebrate the improvements and note where you struggled. Adjust the next month's plan accordingly.

Avoid Perfectionism

Financial management is a learning process. You might slip up and make an impulsive buy or forget a due date occasionally. The key is to notice the slip, fix it if possible, and move on. Beating yourself up will not help. Focus on small steady gains.

Look for More Tips

From podcasts to blogs, there are many resources on budgeting and debt reduction. If you find one that speaks in a clear way that fits your learning style, follow it. Keep looking for small but meaningful tips you can add to your routine.

Conclusion of Chapter 11

Money management can be one of the most stressful parts of adult life, especially for men with ADHD. The good news is that practical methods—like using simple budgets, automating bills, cutting back on impulsive purchases, and setting realistic savings goals—can make a big difference. You do not have to rely on willpower alone. With the right systems and tools in place, you can develop healthier financial habits.

Remember that progress may be gradual, and slip-ups are part of the process. Each time you pay a bill on time, skip an unnecessary purchase, or add to your savings, you are building a more stable future. Over time, you may find that the anxiety around finances lessens, allowing you to channel energy into the parts of life that matter most—family, friends, work, and personal growth. Good money habits will not solve all challenges, but they remove a major source of stress, giving you more peace of mind and freedom to focus on what truly matters.

Chapter 12: Routines, Sleep, and Taking Care of Yourself

Introduction

Life with ADHD can be hectic. Men might race from one obligation to another, forget regular tasks, skip meals, and lose sleep. Without a solid routine, everything can feel disorganized. On top of that, many men with ADHD battle fatigue, struggle to maintain consistent sleep, and ignore basic self-care. This can worsen ADHD signs, creating a cycle of low energy, bad moods, and fuzzy thinking.

This chapter focuses on the value of routines, the importance of sleep, and how basic self-care can help men with ADHD feel more balanced. You do not need a perfect routine to see benefits. Even small changes in daily habits can add structure that reduces chaos. When you sleep well, eat properly, and take steps to limit stress, you have a stronger foundation for everything else—your job, your family life, and your mental health.

Why Routines Help ADHD

1. Reducing Mental Clutter

When you have set times to do everyday tasks—like waking up, eating meals, or showering—you eliminate the need to plan them over and over. This frees your mind to focus on more pressing tasks. Routines bring predictability, which can calm the ADHD brain.

2. Less Time Lost to Procrastination

If you know that at 8 PM, you do a quick cleanup of your bedroom, you are less likely to leave it in a mess for days. When tasks happen at the same time each day or week, there is less decision-making about "when" to do them. This reduces the chance of endless postponing.

3. Building Momentum

Once you complete one routine step, it is easier to move to the next. A morning routine might go like this: get up, take a shower, get dressed, make breakfast, check your planner. Each step flows into the next with little extra thought. This momentum can keep you from stalling in bed or wandering around unfocused.

4. Stability for Emotional Health

Life can feel overwhelming when ADHD signs flare up. Routines act like an anchor, giving you a few things you can control every day. This sense of stability can lower stress and help you handle surprises better.

Creating a Basic Routine

Morning Routine

A good day often starts the night before, with a consistent bedtime. But let us focus on the morning itself:

1. **Same Wake-Up Time**: Try to get up around the same time each day, even on weekends if possible. This keeps your body's internal clock more stable.
2. **Avoid Phone Glare Immediately**: Checking your phone first thing can suck you into emails or social media. Consider waiting until after you have fully woken up.
3. **Hydration and Light Meal**: Drinking water soon after waking helps you feel more alert. A simple, balanced breakfast offers steady energy.
4. **Quick Review of the Day**: Look at your planner or list of tasks to know what is coming. This reduces morning confusion about what you should do next.

Work or Daytime Routine

If you have a job, you probably have some structure already. You can still add small routines:

1. **Lunch Break Reminder**: Men with ADHD might forget to eat if they get hyperfocused. Set an alarm for lunch, or schedule a mid-day meal in your calendar.
2. **Short Stretch Breaks**: Take 2-3 minute breaks every couple of hours to stretch or walk. This not only helps with restlessness but also refreshes your mind.
3. **Designated Times for Email**: Instead of constantly checking email, set blocks (e.g., morning, midday, late afternoon). This prevents distraction and helps you stay in control.

Evening Routine

1. **Wind-Down Period**: Turn off bright screens at least 30 minutes before bed. Harsh light from phones or laptops can disrupt sleep hormones.
2. **Plan for Tomorrow**: Look at your schedule for the next day, lay out clothes, and set out items you will need (like keys, wallet). This lowers morning stress.
3. **Relaxation**: Engage in a calming activity—light reading, gentle stretches, or listening to soft music. This signals your brain to slow down for sleep.
4. **Consistent Bedtime**: Going to bed at about the same time each night helps regulate your body clock.

Managing Sleep Problems

The ADHD-Sleep Link

Men with ADHD often have irregular sleep patterns. Some stay up late because their minds keep racing, or they may hyperfocus on a hobby or the internet deep into the night. Lack of sleep can worsen focus and impulse control the next day, fueling a vicious cycle.

Tips for Better Sleep

1. **Limit Caffeine Later in the Day**: Caffeine can linger in your system, making it hard to wind down at night. Consider cutting off caffeinated drinks by mid-afternoon.
2. **Create a Sleep Sanctuary**: Keep your bedroom cool, dark, and quiet. If outside noise is a problem, use earplugs or a white noise machine.
3. **Unwind Before Bed**: Practice brief relaxation methods, like deep breathing or progressive muscle relaxation. This helps calm a busy mind.
4. **Avoid Heavy Meals Close to Bed**: Eating a large meal right before bedtime can disrupt digestion and sleep quality.

Combatting Late-Night Hyperfocus

Some men find they are most awake at night, leading them to dive into games, shows, or reading until very late. If you need to shift to a more typical schedule, set a strict cutoff time for evening activities. You could set an alarm at 10 PM reminding yourself it is time to start winding down. This might be tough initially, but over time your body can adjust.

Naps: Helpful or Harmful?

A short, 20-minute power nap in the early afternoon can be refreshing. But long naps or late-day naps might ruin nighttime sleep. If you struggle to sleep at night, skip naps altogether or keep them brief and before mid-afternoon.

Nutrition and Eating Habits

Steady Energy Sources

Skipping meals or eating random junk can lead to crashes in energy and attention. Men with ADHD often do well with meals or snacks that include protein and complex carbohydrates. Examples: eggs and whole-grain toast for breakfast, chicken salad for lunch, nuts or yogurt as a snack.

Meal Prep

If cooking every day feels overwhelming, consider meal prepping once or twice a week. Prepare large batches of simple dishes—like grilled chicken, rice, and veggies—and store them in portioned containers. This reduces daily cooking tasks and keeps you from grabbing unhealthy fast food out of impulse.

Setting Alarms for Meals

It might sound odd to set an alarm to eat, but if you are the type who forgets lunch until 3 PM, an alarm can help. Hunger can sneak up and cause irritability or poor focus. By planning meals, you keep your energy more stable.

Limiting Sugar

Sugary treats or drinks give a quick rush but lead to a crash afterward. This crash can worsen ADHD signs. Aim for balanced snacks instead, such as fruit with some cheese, or a protein bar that is not loaded with sugar.

Exercise and Movement

Benefits for ADHD

Exercise can help improve focus and mood. It releases chemicals in the brain that support attention. Men with ADHD may notice they feel calmer and more alert after a workout. Physical activity can also reduce restlessness.

Finding the Right Activity

Pick something you actually enjoy. That might be weightlifting, running, hiking, dancing, or a team sport. If you force yourself to do an activity you hate, you will likely quit. Start small—take a 15-minute walk each day—and build from there.

Scheduling Workouts

If you do not block out time for exercise, it is easy for it to disappear from your day. Treat it like an appointment. Write it in your planner: "6 PM: Walk or jog for 20 minutes." This helps you make exercise a habit rather than an afterthought.

Pairing Exercise with Routine

If possible, combine exercise with another routine you already have. For instance, if you pick up your child from school every day, maybe head to the park afterward for a short walk. This way, it becomes part of your normal cycle of tasks.

Handling Stress and Overwhelm

Identifying Stress Triggers

Men with ADHD might feel overwhelmed by constant demands, disorganized spaces, or unexpected changes. Take note of what sets off your stress. Is it a cluttered environment, tight deadlines, or conflict at home? Recognizing triggers lets you create strategies to reduce or avoid them.

Short Stress Breaks

During a busy day, pause for 2 minutes to do a quick tension release. You could close your eyes, take a few deep breaths, roll your shoulders, and let out a slow exhale. This mini-reset can stop stress from building into frustration or anger.

Mindful Activities

Simple mindfulness habits can help you stay grounded. For example, when washing dishes, focus on the warmth of the water and the smell of the soap instead of letting your mind race. Such mindful moments teach your brain to slow down and notice the present.

Saying "No" Sometimes

Men with ADHD can get excited about new ideas or feel pressured to help everyone. This can lead to an overloaded schedule. Learning to politely decline requests or tasks can protect your time and energy. If you struggle with saying "no," practice phrases like "I need to check my schedule first" or "I can't take that on right now."

Grooming and Personal Care

Benefits of a Personal Care Routine

Keeping up with grooming and cleanliness can seem small, but it boosts self-confidence and reduces stress. A quick shower, shaving routine, and dressing in clean clothes give a sense of order. This may also help you feel more prepared for work or social events.

Setting Reminders

If you forget tasks like brushing teeth or taking medication at the right time, set phone alerts or put sticky notes on your bathroom mirror. Consistency is key; doing the same grooming tasks in the same order each day reduces the chance of forgetting.

Simplify Choices

Some men with ADHD waste time picking outfits or deciding which hair product to use. If you find yourself stuck in decision paralysis, reduce options. For instance, limit your wardrobe to easy-to-match clothes or pick one hair product that works best for daily use.

Digital Detox and Device Management

Phone Use Boundaries

Smartphones are a blessing and a curse. They can remind you of important tasks, but also suck you into social media or games. Set certain rules for yourself, such as "No phone during meals" or "No social media after 9 PM."

App Limits

Many devices let you set daily time limits on certain apps. If you find that you lose hours scrolling through feeds, consider using these built-in tools. When the time limit is reached, the app locks for the day unless you manually override it.

Tech-Free Periods

Try having at least one period a day, maybe an hour in the evening, when you step away from all screens. Use this time to read a physical book, talk with family, or just unwind. This can calm the mind, making it easier to sleep later.

Social and Emotional Self-Care

Nurturing Friendships

While routines are about structure, self-care is also about building healthy social bonds. Men with ADHD sometimes isolate themselves if they feel overwhelmed. Making time to see friends or talk by phone can boost mood and give you a break from daily stress.

Relaxing Activities

It is easy to overlook hobbies when life is busy. But doing something you enjoy—like drawing, playing an instrument, or tinkering with a personal project—helps recharge your mental batteries. If you can schedule a brief hobby time each week, that can be a significant emotional boost.

Monitoring Mood

If you notice you are feeling down or anxious often, do not brush it aside. Mood issues can show up alongside ADHD, especially if life feels chaotic. Considering talking to a counselor or seeking support. Sometimes, adjusting a daily routine or learning a coping method can improve mood significantly.

Balancing Work and Personal Time

Clear Boundaries

If work spills into your evenings and weekends, you might never get real downtime. Try to set a cut-off hour for work emails or tasks, unless your job absolutely requires being on call. This helps you protect your personal space for rest and family.

Prioritize Tasks

Do not overload each day with too many tasks. Pick the most important ones (maybe 3-5) and focus on those. If you finish them, anything else is a bonus. This approach keeps you from feeling like a failure when a giant to-do list goes unfinished.

Use Alarms for Transitions

If you need to leave work by 6 PM to pick up your kids, set an alarm at 5:45 PM so you can wrap up. Men with ADHD can get so lost in tasks that they lose track of time. Regular alarms are a safety net.

Adjusting Routines Over Time

Stay Flexible

Routines should serve you, not control you. Life changes—new job, new home, or shifting family needs—may require you to tweak your schedule. That is fine. Think of routines as a framework that can evolve as you do.

Track What Works and What Fails

After a few weeks, look at your daily or weekly routines. Are there spots where you are constantly slipping up or skipping tasks? Maybe your bedtime is too early for your natural night-owl tendencies, or your morning tasks take longer than you scheduled. Adjust accordingly.

Celebrate Small Wins

When you manage to stick to a new routine for a week or two, acknowledge that progress (maybe give yourself a small treat or a mental pat on the back). This reinforces the positive behavior. Consistency is easier when you see it paying off in better focus, calmer moods, or more free time.

Self-Care Beyond Routines

Medical Check-Ups

Men sometimes ignore doctor visits or dental check-ups. But staying on top of medical care can catch small issues before they become big. Regular check-ups also keep track of your overall health, which can impact ADHD signs.

Mental Health Support

ADHD often comes with stress, anxiety, or sadness. If you notice these feelings affecting your life, consider talking to a counselor or a support group. Therapy sessions can teach coping skills for stress, while group settings let you see you are not alone.

Mindful Breathing or Relaxation

Set aside 5 minutes a day for calm breathing. Sit in a quiet spot, close your eyes, and inhale slowly through your nose, then exhale through your mouth. Focus on the sensation of air moving in and out. Even a brief session can help reset a busy mind.

Conclusion of Chapter 12

Routines, adequate sleep, and basic self-care form the groundwork for tackling ADHD challenges. With a structured but flexible approach, you can handle day-to-day life more smoothly and reduce the chaos that often shadows men with ADHD. Simple routines—like having a consistent bedtime, scheduling short breaks, and planning meals—can help you stay on top of your schedule rather than feeling like you are constantly playing catch-up.

A good night's rest is also crucial. Even though ADHD can make it hard to settle down at night, steps like avoiding late caffeine, dimming screens, and winding down with calming activities can significantly improve sleep quality. Along with healthy eating, regular exercise, and stress management, these habits give your mind and body a more stable base.

Taking care of yourself does not have to be complicated or time-consuming. Small shifts—like setting alarms to remember lunch, blocking out time for a quick walk, or building a short wind-down routine before bed—can have real effects on your day. By putting self-care at the center, you build a stronger foundation that supports your work, relationships, and mental well-being. And in doing so, you set yourself up for a healthier, more balanced life with ADHD.

Chapter 13: Fatherhood and Family Duties

Introduction

Becoming a father is a huge responsibility and can bring both joys and struggles. For men with ADHD, the daily tasks of parenting may be more challenging. Routines, planning, and discipline are key parts of fatherhood, but these can clash with ADHD signs such as forgetfulness, impulsiveness, or trouble staying organized. Still, there are ways to handle these challenges and form strong connections with your children.

This chapter offers guidance for men with ADHD who are fathers. It covers day-to-day duties, balancing work and home life, and healthy ways to connect with your children. Even if some parts feel overwhelming, small steps and practical strategies can ease the strain. By knowing your personal needs and using specific tools, you can become more engaged and reliable for your kids, your partner, and yourself.

Unique Challenges of Fatherhood with ADHD

1. **Lack of Time Awareness**: Fathers often need to switch between work duties, picking up kids, attending sports events, and helping with homework. Men with ADHD may lose track of time or struggle to transition smoothly from one responsibility to another.
2. **Overstimulation**: Kids can be loud, messy, and unpredictable. This might trigger restlessness or frustration if you already find it hard to focus or manage emotions.
3. **Impulsive Reactions**: Dealing with children's misbehavior or noise could lead to sudden outbursts if you do not have a good handle on emotional control.
4. **Forgetting Important Dates or Tasks**: A child's doctor appointment or school project due date can slip your mind if you do not have a solid reminder system. This can cause tension with your partner and disappoint your child.

5. **Difficulty Consistent Discipline**: Being consistent with rules can be hard if you feel disorganized or if you get distracted easily. One day you might enforce a rule strictly, the next day you might forget about it entirely.

Understanding that these challenges are linked to ADHD can help you form a plan. It is not about being a bad father—rather, it is about figuring out tactics to handle those areas where ADHD can get in the way.

Setting Clear Family Routines

Morning Routine for the Whole Family

- **Wake-Up Time**: If your children have to get to school by a certain hour, set a family wake-up time that gives enough margin for breakfast and dressing.
- **Visual Schedules**: Create a simple chart showing each morning step: wake up, wash face, get dressed, eat breakfast, and so on. This can help you and your children stay on track.
- **Divide Tasks**: If you share parenting with a partner, decide who handles which part of the routine. Maybe you help with breakfast while your partner preps lunches, or vice versa.

After-School Routine

- **Check-In Period**: When kids come home, spend a short time hearing about their day. This helps you transition from work mode to father mode.
- **Homework Spot**: Set a consistent place for homework. If you also need to complete some job tasks at home, you could work side by side with your child in a quiet room (if both tasks allow it).
- **Snack and Play**: Kids need some free time, and you might need a short mental break too. Setting a half-hour for snack and play can let both of you recharge before the evening's responsibilities.

Bedtime Routine

- **Wind-Down Activities**: Reading a story, giving younger children a bath, or having a quiet chat can help calm your kids. It also helps you slow down from the day's hustle.
- **Regular Lights-Out**: Aim for a set bedtime. If you also struggle with late nights, this can motivate you to shut down distractions at a reasonable hour.
- **Prepare for Next Day**: Teach children to lay out clothes or pack schoolbags before bed. You can do the same for your own work items. This practice reduces morning stress.

Handling Emotional Overload

Recognize Triggers

If you find yourself getting irritated at small things—like a spilled glass of milk or a noisy TV—it may be a sign you are at your stress limit. Notice physical signs: a tight jaw, shallow breathing, or feeling hot. Once you see these signals, pause and try to calm down before reacting.

Cool-Down Strategy

Taking a brief break can prevent outbursts. For example, if your child is arguing with you, step away for 30 seconds to breathe deeply. This short gap can help you choose a calmer response. Let your child know you will return to talk it through.

Be Honest About Feelings

Children often sense tension, so trying to hide all negative emotions might confuse them. You can say, "Daddy feels upset right now, so I need a moment to think." This teaches them that taking a short pause to handle frustration is normal, not a sign of weakness.

Apologize When Needed

If you do blow up, apologize after you have cooled down. It is important for kids to see that adults can make mistakes and then correct them. A simple, "I'm sorry I shouted earlier. I was frustrated, but I should have handled it better," goes a long way in restoring trust.

Involving Yourself Actively

One-on-One Time

Plan short periods of individual time with each child. This can be a quick walk, reading together, or doing a puzzle. These moments help you learn more about your child's interests and build a deeper bond, which can sometimes get lost in the chaos of daily life.

Find Shared Activities

Look for hobbies or interests you and your kids can do together—like building models, playing sports, or cooking. This is a natural way to keep your ADHD mind engaged while also strengthening relationships.

Attend School Events and Activities

Try to show up for parent-teacher meetings, school performances, or sports games. Set calendar reminders well in advance. Even if you can only stay for part of an event, your presence shows support and helps you stay up-to-date on your child's experiences.

Support Their Interests

If your child loves art, encourage that passion, even if it is not your personal favorite activity. Ask questions about their artwork or consider displaying it at home. Showing interest in your child's hobbies can foster closeness and give them a sense of pride.

Sharing Duties with Your Partner

Clear Communication

ADHD can cause confusion if both partners assume the other has handled a task. Talk openly about who is responsible for what. You might use a shared online calendar or list to keep track of tasks like grocery shopping, picking up kids, or paying certain bills.

Respecting Each Other's Strengths

If you are good at cooking but terrible at remembering deadlines, maybe you handle dinners while your partner handles school forms. Balancing responsibilities based on strengths and weaknesses lowers conflict and helps the household run more smoothly.

Scheduled Check-Ins

A weekly check-in with your partner—maybe Sunday evenings—can help you discuss upcoming events, any issues with the kids, and overall family plans. This short, structured conversation reduces last-minute surprises.

Dealing with Tension

If you sense ongoing friction, it might be worth seeking couples counseling or parenting support. Many men with ADHD find that a neutral party can help them and their partner communicate better and solve issues before they escalate.

Strategies for Discipline

Consistency Is Key

Children thrive on predictable rules and responses. For men with ADHD, consistency can be hard. Try using written rules. For example, if the rule is "No screen time until homework is done," make sure you apply that every day. When you feel tempted to change the rule on a whim, remind yourself that inconsistency confuses kids.

Simple Consequences

When a rule is broken, keep the consequence short and clear. If the child does not do chores, they lose 30 minutes of screen time or get an extra chore. Avoid complicated punishments that you might forget or fail to track. The simpler, the better.

Positive Reinforcement

Praising good behavior is often more effective than focusing on mistakes. If your child cleans their room without nagging, acknowledge it: "I like how you put your toys away. Thank you!" This makes them more likely to repeat that behavior.

Logical vs. Emotional Response

Try to handle discipline logically rather than with raw anger. If you are too frustrated to think clearly, take a short pause. Then, explain the consequence calmly. This method shows your kids that rules are based on fairness, not just your mood.

Managing Homework and School Support

Shared Study Time

If you struggle with focusing, doing homework alongside your child in a quiet space can help both of you. You can work on your own tasks, like reading or bills, while your child tackles homework. This models discipline and reduces their loneliness.

Breaking Big Tasks Into Steps

Kids with big projects might also feel overwhelmed. Teach them the same methods that can help adults with ADHD: list the steps, spread them over several days, and celebrate each small milestone. This approach reduces last-minute chaos.

Communication with Teachers

Let your child's teacher know if you have specific days that are harder for you to be involved, such as a busy work schedule. Many teachers appreciate knowing the family's situation so they can adapt communication methods or offer extra reminders.

Use Tools

Set phone alarms for important school deadlines or tests. If your child has online resources, bookmark them. Keeping a designated homework folder and checking it daily prevents lost assignments.

Handling Multiple Kids

Individual Attention

If you have more than one child, each has unique needs. Creating small windows of personal time with each child can help. Even 10 minutes of focused interaction can strengthen your connection.

Delegating Responsibilities

Older kids can sometimes help with younger siblings. This does not mean dumping all tasks on them, but simple chores like reading a bedtime story to a younger sibling can free you to handle another child's need. Just be fair and balanced in your approach.

Family Meetings

Some families hold short weekly meetings where everyone, including kids, talks about schedules, upcoming events, or issues at home. This can be a constructive way to address conflicts or plan fun outings.

Teaching ADHD Awareness to Your Children

Open Discussions

If you feel it is appropriate, explain ADHD to your kids in simple terms: "Dad's brain sometimes jumps around, so I need to use certain methods to keep track of things." Children often handle this information well if it is clear and not presented with shame.

Leading by Example

When your kids see you using lists, calendars, or alarms, they learn strategies for handling their own tasks. Over time, they might pick up these methods themselves, especially if they notice them working for you.

Avoid Blaming ADHD for Everything

While it is good to acknowledge ADHD, try not to use it as an excuse for every mistake or conflict. Instead, show your children that you are actively finding ways to improve, and sometimes you will correct yourself when ADHD signs pop up. This teaches them accountability and resilience.

Balancing Work and Fatherhood

Work Schedules

If your job has flexible options, see if you can adjust hours or work remotely on certain days to be more available for your kids. For men with ADHD, a more adaptable schedule can help reduce stress and give you time for family commitments.

Setting Clear Boundaries

Try to avoid bringing work stress home if possible. Turn off work emails during family time, if your position allows it. A mental boundary between work and home can keep you from being too distracted when your kids need your attention.

Self-Care for Energy

Fatherhood plus work can be draining. Men with ADHD need to protect their energy to stay patient with children. Ensure you are getting enough sleep, exercise, and healthy meals to avoid burnout. If you are exhausted, it is harder to handle kids' needs calmly.

Co-Parenting After a Separation or Divorce

Consistent Routines Across Homes

If you share custody with an ex-partner, try to keep certain basic routines the same in both households—like bedtime or homework rules. This consistency helps your child feel secure and reduces confusion.

Civil Communication with the Other Parent

Conflict between parents can affect children's emotional health. Even if you and your ex-partner have disagreements, try to keep communication polite and about the children's needs. Tools like shared calendars or co-parenting apps can help track schedules.

Managing Guilt

Some divorced fathers with ADHD feel guilty about not being around 24/7. Focus on making the time you do have count. Activities, honest talks, and consistent support matter more than trying to be perfect.

Extended Family Involvement

Grandparents, Aunts, and Uncles

Relatives can provide extra support, whether it is babysitting, helping with school pickups, or offering a place for the kids to spend a weekend afternoon. Accepting help can ease your load, but make sure everyone respects boundaries and parenting decisions.

Keeping Track of Events

Family gatherings, birthdays, and holidays can pile up on your calendar. Use the same scheduling methods—alarms, shared calendars—to avoid letting important family events slip by. Consistent attendance at family get-togethers shows your kids the value of extended family bonds.

Clarifying Parenting Choices

Some relatives might not understand ADHD or your parenting style. Friendly, concise explanations can reduce tensions. Stand firm if they question your rules or methods, but try to do so calmly. Respect can go both ways when they see you are doing your best.

Taking Care of Yourself as a Father

Physical Health Check

Regular checkups, exercise, and a decent diet boost your energy and mood. If you ignore your body, stress and ADHD signs can get worse. Sometimes, it feels like you do not have time, but small routines (like a short morning walk) can keep you more present for your kids.

Mental Health

If you have ongoing stress, anxiety, or low mood, consider talking to a counselor or joining a support group for fathers. Many men with ADHD also find therapy useful for learning parenting strategies. This can help break negative cycles and offer fresh ideas for handling family duties.

Hobbies and Relaxation

Yes, fathers are busy, but having a hobby or some personal time can keep you from feeling trapped in constant obligations. It might be a weekly sports league, reading before bed, or working on a personal project. Balancing personal interests with fatherhood can help you recharge.

Teaching Responsibility to Your Kids

Household Chores

Encourage children to take on age-appropriate chores. This not only helps you but teaches them life skills. Simple tasks like clearing the table, sorting laundry, or feeding a pet can give your kids a sense of contribution.

Consequences for Unfinished Tasks

Be fair but firm. If chores are not done, calmly enforce a fitting consequence. This helps your kids learn accountability, and it also reduces the chance that you end up doing everything in a rush.

Rewarding Follow-Through

When children finish chores without prodding, give verbal praise or a small privilege (like extra reading time). Positive feedback can motivate them to continue helping out.

Handling Special Situations

Children with ADHD

There is a chance your child may have ADHD too, as it can run in families. If you suspect this, consider talking to a specialist for a proper evaluation. This does not mean your child will have the same experiences you did, but early awareness can help you both navigate challenges together.

Special Events and Vacations

Planning large outings, like vacations, can be stressful for a father with ADHD. Use checklists, plan ahead, and involve the children in packing. Build in downtime during the trip so you are not overwhelmed by non-stop activity.

Illness or Emergencies

Unexpected emergencies—like a child getting sick—can throw your routine off. Keep a list of key contacts (doctors, neighbors, close relatives) easily accessible, perhaps in your phone and printed on the fridge. This reduces panic when quick action is needed.

Looking to the Future

Adapting as Kids Grow

As your children move from toddlers to teens, your parenting approach may shift. Older kids might need more emotional support and fewer direct rules. Stay open to adjusting your methods and keep communication lines open, even if teen years become bumpy.

Teaching Independence

Help your kids learn to manage their own tasks, schedules, and responsibilities. This not only makes them more prepared for adult life but also eases your load. Let them make small choices and handle minor consequences as they mature.

Celebrating Progress

Whenever you see improvements—like fewer missed events or calmer reactions to conflicts—acknowledge it. Recognizing progress encourages you to keep applying ADHD strategies in family life. It also shows your kids that you are dedicated to growing as a parent.

Chapter 14: Communication Skills and Conflict Handling

Introduction

Good communication is the backbone of healthy relationships, whether with family, friends, or coworkers. For men with ADHD, staying focused in a conversation can be harder than it looks. You might interrupt without realizing, miss key details, or get frustrated quickly if things turn tense. Conflict, in turn, can escalate because impulsive words come out before you think them through.

This chapter focuses on ways to improve communication and handle conflicts more smoothly. You will learn practical tips for active listening, speaking clearly, and responding calmly when disagreements arise. While perfection is not the goal, every step to improve how you talk and listen can strengthen bonds and reduce needless tension. Whether it is with a spouse, a child, a friend, or a boss, better communication methods can make a lasting difference.

Common Communication Barriers with ADHD

1. **Distracted Mind**: You might zone out if the conversation goes long or if multiple thoughts bounce around in your head.
2. **Impulsive Speech**: Blurting out a comment, finishing someone else's sentence, or shifting topics abruptly can happen if you struggle with self-control.
3. **Memory Gaps**: You might forget what was said earlier in the conversation or lose track of the main point.
4. **Emotional Reactivity**: If you feel criticized, you could jump into defense mode or anger before understanding the other person's perspective.

These patterns can create misunderstandings. The person you are speaking with might feel ignored or think you are not interested. You might feel they are talking too slowly or are not getting to the point. Recognizing these patterns is the first step toward better communication.

Active Listening Techniques

1. Maintain Eye Contact

Looking at the speaker—without staring intensely—helps you stay engaged. It also signals that you are paying attention. If you find it uncomfortable to look directly at their eyes, aim your gaze at the space between their eyes or at their forehead.

2. Use Verbal and Nonverbal Feedback

Nod occasionally or say, "I see," or "Yes," to show you are following. These small cues keep you from drifting into your own thoughts. They also let the speaker know you are still with them.

3. Paraphrase

After someone explains a point, repeat it in your own words: "So, you are upset because the project deadline was changed, and no one told you?" This method helps confirm you heard them correctly and clarifies any confusion.

4. Ask Questions

If something is unclear, ask: "Can you clarify what you mean by that?" or "When did that happen?" Questions keep you active in the conversation. They also show the speaker that you genuinely want to understand.

Speaking Clearly

1. Organize Thoughts Before Speaking

Take a brief moment to figure out your main point. If you start talking without clarity, you might bounce from topic to topic, confusing the listener. It can help to jot down a note if it is an important discussion.

2. Keep It Brief and Focused

Men with ADHD might go off on tangents. Try to stick to one issue at a time. If you notice you are drifting, pause and bring the talk back to the main topic.

3. Use "I" Statements

When expressing concerns, say "I feel" or "I noticed" instead of "You always" or "You never." For example, "I feel overlooked when I do not get any feedback," rather than, "You never listen to me." This approach reduces blame and helps prevent the other person from becoming defensive.

4. Watch Your Tone

Your voice tone can change the meaning of what you say. Speaking in a calm, steady voice usually works better than raising your voice or sounding sarcastic. If you sense anger creeping in, consider taking a short break to reset.

Handling Interruptions and Impulses

1. Use a Wait Time

If you often interrupt people, try counting silently to two after someone stops speaking. This pause helps you confirm they are done before you speak. Also, if a new thought pops into your head mid-conversation, jot it down briefly so you can return to it when it is your turn to speak.

2. Physical Reminders

Some men with ADHD find it helpful to keep a small object in their hand, like a stress ball or pen. Squeezing the object can help direct restless energy and remind you to hold back any impulsive remarks.

3. Apologize if You Cut Someone Off

If you do interrupt, just say, "Sorry, I interrupted. Please go on." It shows respect and helps the flow of conversation return to the other person's point.

4. Practice Turn-Taking

If a discussion involves multiple people, focus on each speaker and wait for a clear gap. Mentally track who is speaking and who is next. If it is a formal setting, raise your hand or signal that you would like to speak.

Conflict Basics

1. Identify the Real Issue

Conflicts can escalate if the main problem is not recognized. For example, if you are angry at your partner for criticizing your lateness, think deeper: Are you really upset about the comment on lateness, or do you feel disrespected in general? Identifying the core issue helps you focus on a real solution.

2. Stay on Topic

During arguments, men with ADHD might jump to unrelated complaints or bring up old problems. This can make the conflict messy. Stick to the current issue. If other topics are important, handle them later, one at a time.

3. Control Your Volume

When voices rise, the other person may feel attacked. If you notice you are yelling or your partner is yelling, suggest taking a calm break. Say something like, "Let's step away and talk in 10 minutes." A short pause can cool tensions before continuing.

4. Seek Win-Win Solutions

Conflict is not about winning or losing. Try to find outcomes that address both sides' concerns. For instance, if you want more time for a personal hobby but your partner wants you to be present at certain family events, you could schedule a specific hobby time on weekends and commit to being fully available on certain evenings.

Steps to Resolve Conflict

1. **Listen and Let the Other Person Finish**: Do not plan your rebuttal while they talk. Focus on understanding.
2. **Summarize**: Reflect back what you heard to confirm correctness.
3. **Explain Your Perspective**: Calmly describe your feelings or needs.
4. **Brainstorm Solutions**: Propose ideas. Let the other person propose ideas. Keep an open mind.
5. **Agree on Action**: Choose a solution together.
6. **Follow Up**: Check in later to see if the solution is working. If it is not, adjust as needed.

Emotional Control in Difficult Talks

Recognizing Triggers

Does a certain phrase or tone set you off? Maybe you get defensive if someone mentions your forgetfulness. Being aware of triggers helps you pause and respond more calmly.

Breathing Methods

A few deep breaths can slow a racing heart and give you a moment to gather your thoughts. This can reduce the chance of snapping back with harsh words.

Time-Outs

If a conversation is too heated, politely say you need a moment. Walk around the block or get a glass of water. Let the other person know you are not ignoring them; you just need a pause. Aim to return when you can speak without an emotional explosion.

Self-Talk

Quietly tell yourself, "Stay calm, focus on the point, hear them out." Positive self-talk can keep you grounded. This is especially useful when you sense your anger rising or your attention drifting.

Communication in Romantic Relationships

Regular Check-Ins

Instead of waiting for a big blow-up, couples can schedule small check-ins to talk about minor issues before they grow. For men with ADHD, having a set time (like Sunday evening) to discuss concerns or plans can keep communication consistent.

Listening to Your Partner's Feelings

If your partner complains about your disorganization, hear them out fully. See it from their viewpoint: maybe they feel they shoulder extra tasks. Acknowledge their feelings, then suggest ways to improve, like using shared calendars or setting daily reminders.

Expressing Appreciation

It is easy to focus on problems. Make a point to say a genuine "Thank you" or "I appreciate what you did" each day. Positive words can soften tension and remind both of you that the relationship has supportive elements.

Handling Sensitive Topics

If you need to talk about finances or a concern about your partner's behavior, pick a calm moment. Avoid starting such discussions when either of you is rushed or stressed. State the topic clearly, listen, and work toward a joint solution. If it gets too emotional, take a short break.

Workplace Communication Tips

Clarify Instructions

When a boss or coworker gives you directions, restate them to confirm you understand. You might say, "So I should email the client today and finalize the report by Friday?" This reduces mix-ups.

Managing Meetings

Long meetings can be tough if you lose focus. Take short notes to stay engaged. If possible, request an agenda in advance so you know what to expect. Use the agenda to follow along and place a small check mark by each item as it is covered.

Email Etiquette

If you are prone to sending impulsive emails, draft them first in a separate file. Re-read for clarity and tone. Only then, paste it into the email and send. This extra step can prevent misunderstandings or harsh wording.

Conflict with Colleagues

Stay professional. If tension arises, ask for a short private talk. Focus on the issue—maybe a misunderstanding about roles or deadlines—rather than personal attacks. If it cannot be resolved directly, involve a supervisor or HR, but in a calm manner. Emotional outbursts at work can hurt your reputation and career growth.

Social Circles and Friendships

Balancing Talking and Listening

In casual gatherings, be mindful of letting others speak. If you catch yourself rambling about your topic, ask a question about someone else's life or share the floor. This two-way exchange strengthens friendships.

Group Chats or Parties

Men with ADHD may get overwhelmed in big social settings. If you find yourself zoning out, try to focus on one person's conversation at a time. If you need a break, step outside for a few minutes. Let friends know you just need a short pause.

Handling Disagreements with Friends

Small misunderstandings can escalate quickly. If a friend makes a comment that bothers you, calmly address it. Perhaps say, "Hey, that remark upset me a bit. Can we talk about it?" Approach them privately rather than calling them out in a group. This preserves respect on both sides.

Apologize if You Cross the Line

Sometimes, impulsive words slip out, causing hurt feelings. Own it. Saying "I'm sorry I spoke that way" can rebuild trust. Genuine apologies mean you acknowledge the impact and will try to avoid repeating it.

Technology and Communication

Text and Instant Messaging

Written communication can be handy, but tone is often lost. If a conversation gets tense via text, suggest a call or video chat to avoid misunderstandings. For short updates, texts are fine. For important or sensitive topics, it is better to speak in person or at least on the phone.

Social Media Interactions

Men with ADHD might impulsively comment on or respond to posts, which can lead to online arguments or confusion. Pause before hitting "send." Ask yourself if the comment is respectful and constructive. Consider stepping away from social media if you feel your mood is getting worse.

Using Apps for Better Communication

Shared calendars, note-taking apps, or group collaboration tools can streamline how you share information with family or colleagues. Instead of trying to remember everything, let the app store the details. Just be sure to check the app regularly and keep notifications turned on.

Improving Communication Over Time

Practice in Low-Stakes Situations

If you are working on not interrupting, practice with casual conversations first—like talking to a neighbor about the weather. Focus on letting them finish. Slowly build confidence.

Role-Playing

Some men with ADHD find it useful to role-play tricky conversations with a friend or counselor. For example, if you need to talk to your boss about a problem, rehearsing can help you choose words carefully. It also helps you plan how to react if they respond with surprise or criticism.

Seek Professional Help

If communication struggles lead to frequent conflicts at home or work, consider therapy or coaching. A counselor can teach more in-depth methods for emotional regulation and communication. Sometimes, couples counseling can fix long-standing patterns of miscommunication.

Track Small Wins

Whenever you handle a heated discussion calmly or listen attentively in a long meeting, make a mental note. Maybe write it down somewhere. Recognizing your progress motivates you to keep refining your approach.

Managing Criticism

Separate Criticism from Personal Worth

ADHD can make you extra sensitive to disapproval. Try to view criticism as an opinion about a specific action, not a judgment on your entire character. Ask follow-up questions: "What aspect did you feel was lacking?" This clarifies if the critique is about a single task or habit.

Respond Calmly

If you get feedback at work or from a friend, take a deep breath before speaking. If you react defensively right away, you might miss helpful points. You can say, "Thanks for telling me. I want to think about it, and then we can talk more."

Fix the Problem

If the criticism is valid—such as missing deadlines—show you are willing to take steps to improve. Create a plan or timeline. This demonstrates accountability and seriousness about changing.

Ignore Harsh Personal Attacks

Sometimes, criticism is delivered in a nasty way. If the person is just being rude or insulting, calmly end the conversation or walk away if it is not productive. Protect your mental well-being. You can address the issue later when both sides are calmer.

Conflict Avoidance vs. Healthy Addressing

Knowing When to Address Issues

Avoiding conflict altogether can lead to bigger blowups later. If something bothers you, it is often better to talk about it early while it is small. Letting resentment build can damage relationships, especially if you or the other person vents frustration in harmful ways.

Polite Confrontation

Confrontation does not have to be aggressive. It can be a polite statement of your feelings or needs: "I noticed that the tone of your emails to me is very short. Is something bothering you?" This opens the door to discussion instead of blame.

Picking the Right Time

Do not start a tough conversation when the other person is rushing out the door or in the middle of dealing with a crisis. Choose a time when both can focus, perhaps a quiet lunch break or after dinner when tasks are done. This increases the odds of a constructive outcome.

Knowing When to Let Go

Not every disagreement requires a big talk. If the issue is small and does not harm the relationship, you can let it pass. Men with ADHD might find themselves wanting to address every annoyance, but constant confrontations can wear others out. Use judgment to see which issues matter most.

Chapter 15: Tools, Apps, and Other Supports

Introduction

In today's digital world, there are many tools that can help men with ADHD stay on track. Whether it is organizing daily tasks, managing appointments, or keeping your mind focused, the right supports can make your days more manageable. Yet, with so many apps and gadgets available, it can be tough to pick the right ones—or to avoid being distracted by the same devices that are meant to help you.

This chapter explores various types of tools that can make everyday life simpler for men with ADHD. These range from traditional aids (like notepads and timers) to advanced apps and smart devices. Each option has strengths and weaknesses, and not everyone will like the same approach. The aim is to find a system or set of tools that fits your lifestyle and uses your natural tendencies to your advantage, rather than fighting them.

Traditional Tools That Still Work

1. Paper Planners and Calendars

For many men with ADHD, a physical planner or wall calendar can be easier to see and remember than digital ones. Hanging a large wall calendar in a visible spot—like above a desk or on the fridge—keeps important dates in your line of sight.

- **Pros**:
    - Visual reminder of key events.
    - No need for Wi-Fi or battery.
    - Writing by hand can help you remember events better.
- **Cons**:
    - If you lose it, you cannot quickly replace it.
    - Harder to set up automatic reminders.

- Might require more manual effort to keep updated.

If you decide to use a paper planner, pick one with enough space to write daily tasks. Some prefer planners that have separate sections for each hour of the day, while others like a simple weekly view. Experiment to find what feels comfortable and not overwhelming.

2. Sticky Notes

Sticky notes are basic but can be powerful. Placing a sticky note on your bathroom mirror or front door can remind you about something vital—like mailing a package or taking your medication.

- **Pros**:
    - Low cost and very visible if placed strategically.
    - Quick to write on.
    - Can be color-coded (for instance, pink for urgent tasks, yellow for daily reminders).
- **Cons**:
    - They can pile up or fall off, creating clutter.
    - You might ignore them if they become too common.

To keep them from losing impact, use sticky notes sparingly for top-level tasks or immediate alerts. If you stick them everywhere, they become background noise.

3. Timers and Alarms

A simple kitchen timer or a basic alarm clock can help you stay focused on tasks in small bursts. Set a timer for 25 minutes (a concept similar to the "Pomodoro Technique"), work until it rings, then take a short break. This breaks a large job into smaller, more manageable blocks of time.

- **Pros**:
    - Easy to use.
    - Creates urgency and a clear start-stop point.
    - Helps limit distractions since you know you only have to focus until the timer rings.
- **Cons**:

- Manual effort required to reset or adjust.
- Not as flexible as a phone app that can track multiple tasks.

If you prefer something a bit more advanced, you can look for timers that vibrate or flash lights if you work in a quiet space or cannot have loud rings.

4. Whiteboards

A whiteboard in your bedroom or office can serve as a space to write daily targets, monthly goals, or important phone numbers. You can quickly erase and update it, which is often easier than crossing out notes in a planner.

- **Pros**:
    - Highly visible, encourages you to review tasks often.
    - Great for brainstorming or mind-mapping.
    - Easy to erase and rewrite.
- **Cons**:
    - Requires physical space on a wall.
    - Writing can become messy if not kept neat.
    - You cannot carry it around unless it is a small portable whiteboard.

Digital Tools and Apps

1. Calendar and Reminder Apps

Most smartphones come with a calendar and reminder system. You can set alerts for meetings, due dates, or personal appointments. Examples include Google Calendar, Apple Calendar, and Microsoft Outlook.

- **Pros**:
    - You can create recurring events (weekly staff meetings, monthly bills).
    - Syncs across devices (phone, computer, tablet).
    - You can add alerts (popup, sound, or email) to remind you ahead of time.
- **Cons**:

- If you are prone to phone distractions, you might get sidetracked by other apps.
- You must remember to check the calendar or else the events remain unseen.

A pro tip is to keep the calendar app on your home screen, so it is the first thing you see when you unlock your phone. Also, consider color-coding (work tasks in one color, personal tasks in another).

2. Task Management Apps

There are many apps designed to help you create to-do lists, set deadlines, and break projects into smaller tasks. Examples include Todoist, Microsoft To Do, and Trello.

- **Pros**:
    - Some have collaboration features for team tasks or shared family duties.
    - You can set priorities, labels, and deadlines.
    - Many offer reminders and progress tracking.
- **Cons**:
    - Might feel overwhelming if you try to track every single thing.
    - Requires discipline to update tasks regularly.

A handy tip is to limit the number of categories or labels. Keep it simple: maybe "Urgent," "Today," and "This Week." Sorting tasks into too many labels can cause confusion. Also, check tasks at least once in the morning and once at night to stay organized.

3. Focus and Distraction-Blocking Apps

For men who struggle with online distractions—browsing social media, checking sports scores, or streaming videos—focus apps can be lifesavers. Examples include Freedom, Cold Turkey, or built-in screen time settings on phones.

- **Pros**:
    - You can block specific sites or apps during work hours.

- o   Helps break the habit of mindless scrolling.
- o   Can set time limits for certain activities.
- **Cons**:
  - o   It is easy to override or turn off if you lack self-control.
  - o   May feel restrictive or irritating at first.

Start by blocking your biggest time-wasters. Some men block social media for a few hours each day to force themselves to focus on work. Remember, the goal is not to eliminate fun, but to control when it happens.

4. Note-Taking and Organization Tools

Apps like Evernote, OneNote, or Google Keep let you store notes, images, and web clips in one place. You can categorize them into notebooks or folders, making them easy to find later.

- **Pros**:
  - o   Access notes across multiple devices.
  - o   Can attach images, audio clips, or PDFs.
  - o   Search function helps you find specific keywords quickly.
- **Cons**:
  - o   Requires a learning curve to set up an organized system.
  - o   Must be careful not to dump random notes without sorting, or it becomes cluttered.

A useful approach is to create a small number of main notebooks (e.g., "Work," "Personal," "Ideas") and then label or tag notes within them. Regularly review and clean out notes to prevent a digital mess.

5. Medication Tracking Apps

If you use ADHD medication, you might benefit from apps that remind you to take doses on schedule. Some also let you record how you feel throughout the day, which can help you and your doctor adjust treatment if needed.

- **Pros**:
  - o   Consistent reminders so you do not miss doses.
  - o   Can track side effects or effectiveness.

- May sync with health data, offering a fuller view of your daily routine.
- **Cons**:
    - Must input data regularly for best results.
    - Overdependence on reminders can happen if you do not also build personal habits.

Look for an app that is simple and does not overload you with features you do not need. The main point is to help you take medication on time and keep a basic log of how you feel.

Smart Home and Tech Gadgets

1. Smart Speakers and Voice Assistants

Devices like Amazon Echo, Google Nest, or Apple HomePod can set alarms, make lists, or play music using voice commands. You might say, "Remind me at 8 AM to pack my laptop," or "Add milk to my grocery list."

- **Pros**:
    - Hands-free convenience.
    - Quick reminders without opening an app.
    - Can control other smart devices, like lights or thermostats.
- **Cons**:
    - Requires stable internet connection.
    - May pick up background noise, leading to misheard commands.
    - Potential distraction if you use it to play music or videos and get sidetracked.

Men with ADHD often find voice assistants helpful because they can set reminders on the fly while they think of them. Just be mindful not to spend too much time exploring non-productive functions.

2. Smartwatches

Smartwatches can vibrate for reminders, show quick updates, and track fitness data. Some men find it easier to glance at their wrist for a notification rather than checking a phone and getting pulled into apps.

- **Pros**:
    - Subtle alerts without loud ringtones.
    - Quick way to check tasks or messages.
    - Many have fitness-tracking features, encouraging healthy habits.
- **Cons**:
    - Smaller screen for reading detailed notes.
    - Can become another source of distraction if you get too many notifications.

Customize your watch's notification settings. If you only get alerts for truly important events (like medication reminders or meeting alerts), it can keep you on track without bombarding you.

3. Smart Lighting and Environmental Controls

ADHD can be worsened by poor lighting or distracting environments. Smart bulbs let you adjust the brightness or color of lights from your phone. You can set them to become dimmer as bedtime approaches, signaling your brain to wind down.

- **Pros**:
    - Helps create a calm atmosphere or a bright work environment as needed.
    - You can schedule lights to turn on or off, which can serve as a cue for routine tasks (like turning on bright lights at wake-up time).
    - Can integrate with voice assistants.
- **Cons**:
    - More costly than regular bulbs.
    - Might feel unnecessary if you are not into tech solutions.

Some men with ADHD appreciate the routine cues: for example, lights shifting to a softer hue at 9 PM to remind them it is time to relax.

Strategies for Effective Use of Tools

1. Start Small

Do not download a dozen apps or buy loads of gadgets at once. Pick one or two areas where you struggle the most—say, remembering appointments or controlling phone time—and focus on solutions for those problems first. Overloading yourself with new tools can become another source of confusion.

2. Keep Notifications Under Control

One big challenge is that constant pings or alerts can worsen ADHD by distracting you. Turn off nonessential notifications. If an app notifies you about every minor change, you might never focus. Instead, let your task or calendar app have priority, while other apps are set to silent or no notification.

3. Regularly Review and Prune

Technology can get cluttered quickly. Schedule a monthly check of your apps and digital tools. Remove or uninstall those you have not used in a while. Declutter your computer desktop. This helps maintain a clean digital workspace, making the tools you do rely on more noticeable.

4. Use Physical and Digital in Tandem

Some men find it helpful to keep a physical planner for an overview of the week and a digital task app for daily checklists. Or you might use a wall calendar for family events but rely on a smartphone alarm to remind you about small tasks. Blending both worlds can give you a backup system.

5. Integrate Tools into Routines

Even the best apps will not help if you forget to check them. Tie your tool use to a routine. For example, open your task app every morning at breakfast, or look at your whiteboard each night before bed. Consistency is what makes these tools effective.

Professional Assistance

1. ADHD Coaches and Organizational Experts

Some coaches specialize in helping people with ADHD set up systems that work for them. They can suggest custom methods, keep you accountable, and track progress.

- **Pros**:
    - Personalized guidance.
    - Regular check-ins push you to maintain habits.
    - Helps you solve immediate problems with structure.
- **Cons**:
    - Often costs money.
    - You need to find a coach with experience in adult ADHD.

If a coach is too pricey, look for group sessions or community centers that offer free or low-cost workshops on organization and time management.

2. Occupational Therapists

An occupational therapist (OT) can provide practical methods to handle daily tasks. They often work with people who have focus or motor skill challenges, helping them adapt their environment.

- **Pros**:
    - Can suggest home/workplace adjustments.
    - Hands-on approach to daily routines.
    - Might teach advanced coping skills for ADHD symptoms.
- **Cons**:
    - Access might require insurance or a referral.

- Sessions may be limited depending on your plan.

3. Technology Consultants

Although not specific to ADHD, some consultants help individuals or businesses pick the right tech solutions. They might guide you on how to set up cloud storage, use certain apps efficiently, or secure your data.

- **Pros**:
    - Speeds up the learning curve for certain tools.
    - Good if you have specific tech questions or if you run a small business.
- **Cons**:
    - Costly if you only need minor help.
    - Not specialized in ADHD, so solutions may not address the root issue of focus and memory.

Supporting Children or Family Members with ADHD Tools

If you have a child or spouse with ADHD, you can share the apps and methods you find helpful. Setting up a shared family calendar or a group to-do list can keep everyone on track. Just keep in mind each person might prefer different techniques.

- **Family Calendar**: Tools like Google Calendar let multiple people access the same schedule. Everyone can see upcoming events.
- **Shared Shopping Lists**: Grocery apps allow everyone to add items. This means fewer trips for forgotten foods.
- **Reward Systems for Kids**: Simple apps exist for tracking chores and rewarding kids with points or small treats when they complete tasks.

Using the same tool set can foster teamwork, but do not force a tool on a family member if it does not match their style. Provide options and see what sticks.

Avoiding Over-Reliance on Technology

Though tech can help, it can also become a crutch or even an addiction. Some men with ADHD fall into the trap of constantly tweaking their systems or browsing new productivity apps rather than actually doing tasks.

- **Watch for Over-Tinkering**: If you spend more time setting up your to-do list than checking items off it, you might be procrastinating.
- **Limit Screen Time**: Ironically, you might need another app or device setting to limit how often you fiddle with your phone.
- **Practice Self-Discipline**: Tools are aids, not magic fixes. You still need effort and discipline to follow through.

Balancing the help from apps and gadgets with real-world habits is key. The goal is to use technology as a supportive tool, not as a replacement for personal responsibility.

Troubleshooting Common Issues

1. "I Forget to Check My Apps"

Set a single phone alarm each day named "Check my tasks" or "Check my planner." This reminder can nudge you to look at your list or calendar. Over time, you might build the habit and no longer need the alarm.

2. "Notifications Distract Me All Day Long"

Fine-tune notification settings. For example, allow your calendar to pop up alerts for events but silence social media. Review your phone's settings carefully. There might be a "Do Not Disturb" mode you can schedule during key focus times.

3. "My Tools Become Cluttered and Outdated"

Schedule a weekly "maintenance" session. Spend 15 minutes removing old tasks, archiving completed items, and making sure your upcoming week is planned. Keeping tools fresh encourages regular use.

4. "I'm Not Sure Which App or System Is Best"

Try a tool for a limited time—say, two weeks. If it feels cumbersome or unhelpful, move on to another. Just be sure not to jump too often. Aim to give each system a fair test. You can also read user reviews or ask friends with ADHD for suggestions.

Self-Care Tools

1. Meditation and Relaxation Apps

Apps like Headspace, Calm, or others can guide short breathing exercises or calming sessions. Even 5 minutes of guided relaxation can reduce stress, which often worsens ADHD signs.

- **Pros**:
    - Easy to follow.
    - Encourages daily mindfulness.
    - Can improve mood and focus over time.
- **Cons**:
    - Requires consistency.
    - Might become another forgotten app if you do not schedule sessions.

2. Workout and Step-Tracking Devices

Fitness trackers or step counters can motivate you to move more. Regular exercise helps manage ADHD by boosting energy and focus. Seeing your step count or workout stats can be a fun way to track progress.

- **Pros**:
    - Immediate feedback on activity levels.

- Can set daily or weekly goals.
- Some models buzz to remind you to stand or move after sitting too long.
- **Cons**:
  - The novelty can wear off if you do not set meaningful goals.
  - Might lead to guilt if you are not meeting the standards you set.

Keep it realistic. If you currently move 2,000 steps a day, do not jump to 10,000 steps overnight. Small, steady increments can be more motivating and less overwhelming.

3. Sleep-Tracking Tools

Adequate sleep is crucial. Apps or devices that track your sleep can show how long you rest and if you are waking up often. Some men with ADHD find it motivating to see patterns—like noticing they sleep poorly if they use their phone late at night.

- **Pros**:
  - Raises awareness of sleep habits.
  - Some devices offer gentle alarms that wake you in a light sleep stage.
  - Can help you adjust bedtime routines.
- **Cons**:
  - Data overload if you overanalyze every detail.
  - Not always 100% accurate in measuring sleep stages.

Use the data as a guide, not a source of stress. Focus on practical steps like setting a regular bedtime or avoiding heavy meals too close to bedtime.

Thinking Long-Term

1. Adapting Tools Over Your Lifespan

As your career or personal life changes, so might your preferences. A man in his 20s might love a certain app, while in his 40s he might rely more on a paper planner. Be open to changing systems when your routines shift.

2. Teaching Others

Once you get comfortable with certain tools, you can share them with peers, coworkers, or family members who also struggle with ADHD-related issues. Spreading effective methods can create a supportive community.

3. Tracking Success

Tools are only as good as the results they bring. After using a system for a month or two, ask yourself: "Am I missing fewer deadlines? Am I feeling less stressed about tasks?" If you see progress, keep going. If not, tweak your approach.

Conclusion of Chapter 15

For men with ADHD, the right combination of tools, apps, and supports can be a real game-changer. From old-school paper planners to high-tech reminders, every solution has pros and cons. The secret is to start with your biggest problem areas and choose one or two tools to address them. Keep things simple, avoid notification overload, and integrate your chosen methods into daily life.

Remember, technology is not a magic cure. You still need discipline, consistent review, and the willingness to adjust if something is not working. Over time, a well-selected group of tools can reduce forgetfulness, curb distractions, and give you more control over your schedule. That sense of control can lower stress and free up mental energy for other parts of life—whether that is family, hobbies, or personal growth. With patience and experimentation, you can build a toolbox that truly fits your life and supports you in managing ADHD challenges day by day.

Chapter 16: Building a Trusted Support Group

Introduction

No one should face the challenges of ADHD alone. A reliable network of friends, family, mentors, and professionals can make a huge difference. Support groups can offer understanding, accountability, and practical tips that you will not get on your own. Also, sharing experiences with people who understand ADHD helps combat the sense of isolation or shame that sometimes comes with the condition.

This chapter covers how to form and maintain a support system that helps you handle daily life with ADHD. You will learn about different types of support—emotional, practical, and informational—and how each can aid you in different areas of life. Building a trusted group is not about leaning on others for everything; rather, it is about acknowledging that ADHD can be less overwhelming when you have help and know where to turn.

Why a Support Network Matters

1. Emotional Encouragement

ADHD can lead to frustration, anxiety, or low self-esteem. Having a person (or several people) who genuinely listen and care can reduce negative feelings. This emotional backing provides a safe space to talk about both struggles and small victories.

2. Accountability

When you have a friend or mentor who checks in on your progress, you are more likely to stick to goals—whether it is meeting work deadlines, following a medication schedule, or controlling spending. Accountability partners can gently push you to keep trying when motivation is low.

3. Sharing Resources and Knowledge

Men with ADHD often discover certain tricks or tools that work well for them. In a support setting, these ideas spread quickly. Someone might suggest an app, a therapist, or a time-management approach you never considered.

4. Reducing Stigma

It helps to see you are not the only one dealing with ADHD difficulties. Talking with others in the same boat normalizes your experiences. You can exchange stories of slip-ups and find humor or relief rather than shame.

Types of Support

1. Family Support

Close family members—parents, siblings, or a spouse—often see your struggles up close. If they are understanding, they can help with reminders, share tasks, or provide emotional backing.

- **Pros**:
    - Typically available daily.
    - Deep personal connection.
    - Familiarity with your habits and triggers.
- **Cons**:
    - Family members might lack knowledge of ADHD or might not believe in it as a real condition.
    - Emotional bonds can lead to heated conflicts if they feel they are taking on extra burden.

Encourage family members to learn about ADHD, perhaps by sharing reputable articles or inviting them to a counseling session. Clear communication about what you need (and do not need) from them is key.

2. Friends

Good friends can offer a listening ear or a fresh perspective. They might help you with practical tasks—like moving apartments or giving feedback on a project—or simply hang out with you when you need a break from stress.

- **Pros**:
    - Often less day-to-day tension than family relationships.
    - Social time can keep you from isolation.
    - Friends can connect you with job leads or other resources.
- **Cons**:
    - If friends do not understand ADHD, they might interpret your forgetfulness or impulsiveness as carelessness.
    - Some may be busy with their own lives, limiting how much they can help.

Choose friends who are patient, supportive, and open-minded. Avoid those who belittle your efforts or push you into unhealthy behaviors (like reckless spending or substance misuse).

3. Romantic Partners

If you have a partner, they can be one of the most significant sources of daily support, especially if you live together. They see your routines (or lack thereof) and can help with tasks like budgeting, scheduling, or household chores.

- **Pros**:
    - Deep personal bond, shared responsibilities.
    - Immediate feedback if something is not working.
    - Emotional comfort in times of stress.
- **Cons**:
    - Partners can feel overwhelmed if they must handle many responsibilities alone.
    - Relationship conflicts can arise if ADHD behaviors (like disorganization) are not addressed.

Frequent, honest communication prevents resentment. Setting boundaries and dividing tasks fairly is essential so the partner does not feel like a caregiver. If arguments about ADHD signs occur often, consider couples counseling for extra guidance.

4. Professional Allies

Therapists, ADHD coaches, counselors, or doctors can offer specialized knowledge. They can help you form coping strategies, track progress, and make decisions about medication or therapy.

- **Pros**:
    - Expert advice rooted in research and experience.
    - Structured approach to problem-solving.
    - Confidential setting to discuss private concerns.
- **Cons**:
    - Can be expensive or limited by insurance.
    - Appointments might not be frequent enough for ongoing daily needs.

Finding a professional who truly understands adult ADHD is important. You might have to try more than one therapist or coach before you find a good match.

5. Peer Support Groups

ADHD-focused support groups—either in person or online—let you connect with others who share similar experiences. These can be hosted at community centers, churches, or through websites and social media platforms.

- **Pros**:
    - Members can relate to ADHD-specific struggles.
    - Group discussions often spark creative solutions and empathy.
    - Provides a sense of belonging and reduces isolation.
- **Cons**:
    - Some groups might be unstructured or dominated by certain personalities.

- Confidentiality can be a concern if you share personal details.

If you cannot find an in-person group in your area, look for online forums or social media groups dedicated to ADHD support. Just stay cautious about advice that is not from professionals. Use your judgment when taking suggestions.

Steps to Build Your Network

1. Identify Your Needs

Ask yourself: "Where do I need the most help?" This could be emotional support, organizing tasks, or accountability for specific goals. Knowing your priorities lets you focus on finding the right people or groups.

2. Start with Existing Contacts

You might already have people in your life who can fill these roles. A friend who is naturally organized could become an accountability buddy. A sibling who has ADHD experience could offer empathy.

3. Seek Local Resources

Check community centers, libraries, or hospitals for listings of ADHD or mental health support groups. Some larger workplaces offer employee assistance programs with counseling sessions or referrals.

4. Explore Online Options

If local resources are scarce, online communities can be very helpful. Look for reputable sites or groups moderated by trained individuals. You can join video-based support meetings if you want real-time discussion.

5. Approach Professionals

If you suspect you need deeper guidance—like therapy, coaching, or medical advice—research providers in your area. Read reviews or ask for recommendations from trusted friends, doctors, or community members.

Maintaining and Growing Your Support System

1. Be Open About ADHD

If you want people to support you effectively, they need to understand what ADHD is and how it affects you. Share basic facts, like the need for reminders or your difficulty focusing on certain tasks. Being open also helps them show empathy instead of misunderstanding your behavior.

2. Ask for Specific Help

Vague requests like, "I need help with everything," can confuse supporters. Instead, say, "I'd really appreciate if you could text me on Mondays to remind me about the staff meeting," or "Can we check in once a week to see if I am keeping up with my budget?"

3. Offer Something in Return

Support should not be one-sided. Even if you cannot repay your friend or family member in the same form, you can offer something else—like helping them with a skill you have, doing small favors, or just being a good listener for them. Balanced relationships thrive.

4. Keep Communication Respectful

Even with loved ones, conflicts or misunderstandings may arise. Stay polite and patient. If tensions do emerge, address them directly rather than letting them fester. Healthy communication keeps your support group strong.

5. Stay in Touch Regularly

If you only call a mentor or friend once every few months, the relationship might fade. Make an effort to maintain contact. A quick text or call can keep the bond alive. Regular contact also means they stay updated on how you are doing.

Boundaries and Healthy Limits

1. Know What You Can Ask For

It is fine to ask a friend to remind you of a weekly event, but it might be too much to expect them to manage your entire schedule. Recognize the difference between helpful support and burdensome demands.

2. Watch for Codependency

If a partner or family member starts doing everything for you—paying bills, scheduling appointments—you might never develop your own coping strategies. Aim for assistance that empowers you, not that leads to dependence.

3. Respect Others' Time and Energy

Supporters have their own lives. If you notice they are stressed or have big personal challenges, it might not be the right moment to lean heavily on them. A short check-in to see how they are doing can show you value their well-being too.

4. Protect Your Privacy

Being open about ADHD does not mean you must share every detail of your life. Choose what to share and with whom. If a colleague or acquaintance asks questions you do not feel comfortable answering, it is okay to keep certain boundaries.

Online Support Communities

1. Forums and Groups

Platforms like Reddit or Facebook have communities where users post questions, share stories, and give tips about ADHD. Reading these can offer a sense of solidarity and spark new solutions.

- **Pros**:
    - Wide range of experiences and tips.
    - Available 24/7.
    - Anonymity can help you open up.
- **Cons**:
    - Anonymous users might give misleading information.
    - Negative or toxic comments can appear in unmoderated spaces.

2. Virtual Meetings

Some organizations host video-based support sessions that follow a group format, similar to in-person gatherings. This can be a safe space to talk without leaving your home.

- **Pros**:
    - Real-time interaction, chance to build closer bonds.
    - Helps if you live far from in-person groups or have limited mobility.
    - Usually moderated, which can reduce chaos.
- **Cons**:
    - Can feel impersonal compared to face-to-face contact.
    - Requires stable internet and a quiet space to join the call.

3. Professional-Led Webinars

Mental health experts sometimes run live online sessions about ADHD coping skills. They may cover topics like time management, emotional control, or parenting tips. These can be paid or free.

- **Pros**:
    - Expert information from qualified individuals.
    - Often includes Q&A segments.
    - Recorded sessions let you revisit the material.
- **Cons**:
    - Usually one-way teaching rather than interactive peer support.
    - You might not get personalized feedback if many attendees are present.

Accountability Partnerships

1. Definition of an Accountability Partner

An accountability partner is someone you regularly report to about your goals and progress. This can be a friend, coworker, or fellow ADHD peer. You set clear targets and check in—maybe daily, weekly, or monthly.

2. How It Works

- **Set Clear Goals**: For instance, "I want to finish my project proposal by Friday."
- **Schedule Check-Ins**: Decide when and how you will communicate—texts, calls, or in-person meetings.
- **Review Results**: Did you meet the target? If not, what got in the way?
- **Encouragement and Adjustments**: The partner offers support, and you both brainstorm ways to do better.

3. Benefits

- **Accountability**: You are less likely to slack off if someone else is expecting an update.
- **Shared Insights**: Your partner might see patterns in your behavior and point them out.
- **Inspiration**: Hearing their progress can motivate you, and vice versa.

4. Potential Pitfalls

- **Mismatch**: If your partner also struggles with consistency, check-ins might not happen.
- **Dependence**: You might rely too much on your partner instead of building self-discipline.

Choose someone who has a schedule and communication style compatible with yours. Be open to adjusting the system if it stops being effective.

Involving Mentors or Role Models

1. Finding a Mentor

A mentor is someone who has walked a path you want to follow—perhaps a successful coworker, a community leader, or even a friend who has conquered challenges similar to yours. Ask if they are willing to share advice or meet occasionally to discuss your progress.

2. Respect Their Time

Mentors often volunteer their knowledge. Be sure to show gratitude. Arrive on time if you set a meeting. Summarize your questions clearly so the mentor can give concise answers.

3. Apply What You Learn

A big mistake is listening to a mentor's advice but never acting on it. After each meeting, identify key takeaways and try to put them into practice. At the next meeting, update them on results or struggles.

4. Mentoring Others

Once you make progress, you could pay it forward by guiding someone else who is newer to handling ADHD. Teaching or advising another person can also reinforce your own coping skills.

Handling Setbacks

1. Expect Ups and Downs

Even with the best support group, you will slip occasionally—missing deadlines or having conflicts. This does not mean your network failed. ADHD management is a journey of learning.

2. Talk About Struggles Early

If you notice you are repeatedly messing up in a certain area, bring it up with your support group. Hiding it or waiting until it becomes a crisis can create bigger problems.

3. Adjust the Approach

Sometimes the group dynamic changes. Perhaps a friend moves away or a coach's schedule becomes too busy. Stay flexible and look for new support if needed. That might mean joining a new group or finding a different mentor.

4. Celebrate Small Progress

It is easy to focus on the negatives. Make an effort to share small wins—like remembering an appointment all week or sticking to a budget for a month. Hearing positive news keeps the group spirit up and shows you are growing.

Balancing Independence and Support

1. Your Own Responsibility

While support is invaluable, remember that your actions are ultimately your own responsibility. If you rely too heavily on others to "save" you from ADHD challenges, you may not develop strong self-management skills.

2. Strengthening Self-Reliance

Over time, aim to build habits that need less external prompting. That might mean turning a friend's reminders into your own phone alerts, or gradually reducing the frequency of accountability check-ins as you become more confident.

3. Gratitude and Reciprocation

When you do achieve better self-management, do not forget to thank those who helped you. If you can assist them in some way—whether it is moral support, advice in your area of expertise, or just a friendly ear—offer it. Supportive relationships thrive on mutual respect and exchange.

Conclusion of Chapter 16

Building and maintaining a trusted support group is one of the smartest things men with ADHD can do. Family members, friends, romantic partners, mentors, and professional advisors each bring something unique to the table. Whether you need emotional encouragement, practical advice, or just someone to listen, a strong network makes the path less lonely.

Remember that creating such a network takes effort. You might have to educate loved ones about ADHD, reach out to local or online communities, and be specific about the kind of help you need. Yet, the payoff is a sense of connection and shared understanding that can keep you from feeling isolated or overwhelmed. While self-reliance is important, having people in your corner can lift you through tough times, hold you accountable, and celebrate your steps forward. Over time, this sense of community can add real strength to your journey with ADHD, helping you handle day-to-day tasks and longer-term goals with greater confidence and less stress.

Chapter 17: Handling Shame, Guilt, and Misunderstandings

Introduction

Men with ADHD often experience feelings of shame or guilt about their struggles. They might think they are letting down family, friends, or coworkers. Sometimes, simple tasks—like paying bills on time or following through on work duties—can slip through the cracks, leading to frustration and self-blame. Outside misunderstandings add to this burden: others may see these lapses as laziness or irresponsibility.

This chapter dives into the sources of shame and guilt for men with ADHD, how misunderstandings can form, and practical ways to handle these tough emotions. A central theme here is recognizing the difference between being at fault for something and having a genuine condition that makes certain tasks harder. While responsibility is still important, shaming yourself or letting others shame you can lead to low self-esteem and more intense ADHD signs. Instead, learning healthy coping strategies can reduce these negative feelings, improve relationships, and keep you from being overwhelmed.

Sources of Shame and Guilt

1. **Unmet Expectations**: Men often feel social pressure to perform well, stay organized, and handle responsibilities with ease. ADHD can cause issues in scheduling, memory, or focus, making it tough to meet these expectations.
2. **Frequent Mistakes**: If you lose track of events or drop the ball on a project, you might apologize repeatedly. Over time, these incidents can lead to a sense of failure or inadequacy.

3. **Childhood Labels**: Some men carry memories of being called lazy, unmotivated, or disruptive in school. Hearing negative labels over and over can stick, shaping how you see yourself.
4. **Comparisons to Others**: Watching peers or coworkers manage tasks smoothly while you struggle can deepen feelings of inferiority. This is even stronger if you do not know they may have their own hidden issues.
5. **Criticism from Loved Ones**: Partners or family members may express frustration about disorganization, late bills, or impulsive actions. Even if the criticisms are accurate, the way they are delivered can trigger shame or guilt.

It is important to distinguish between natural responsibility (owning up to errors or oversights) and harmful shame (viewing yourself as unworthy or bad because of ADHD-related missteps).

How Misunderstandings Arise

1. Limited Awareness of ADHD

Many people do not fully understand ADHD and might dismiss it as an "excuse." They see repeated lateness or forgetfulness and assume it reflects a bad attitude or lack of respect. This lack of knowledge can strain relationships at home or in the workplace.

2. Differences in Communication

Men with ADHD might speak quickly, interrupt unintentionally, or jump between topics, confusing listeners. Misunderstandings form when others assume you are not paying attention or do not value their input.

3. Emotional Outbursts

Stress can lead to sudden anger or irritability, which relatives or friends might interpret as hostility or disrespect. Without knowing about ADHD's effect on emotional regulation, they assume you are just being rude.

4. Inconsistent Performance

When you hyperfocus on something you love, you might excel and produce top-quality work. But with tasks you find dull, you might perform poorly or forget them altogether. Others see this inconsistency as "selective effort" or "choosing when to care."

5. Cultural and Social Expectations

In some communities, men are expected to be extremely organized or to never show vulnerability. ADHD can conflict with these cultural norms, leading to more misunderstandings about your character or capabilities.

The Emotional Toll of Shame and Guilt

Shame and guilt can weigh heavily on mental and emotional health:

- **Low Self-Confidence**: Constantly feeling like you have fallen short can stop you from trying new things or setting goals.
- **Anxiety and Depression**: Over time, negative thoughts can spiral into anxiety or a depressed mood.
- **Isolation**: To hide frequent mistakes, you might avoid social events or responsibilities, fearing more judgment.
- **Strained Relationships**: Loved ones might feel you are pulling away or not investing in the relationship.
- **Defensive Behavior**: Some men respond to repeated shame by lashing out, denying issues, or blaming others.

Understanding these effects is the first step in breaking the cycle. The next sections suggest methods to tackle shame, guilt, and misunderstandings head-on.

Strategies for Overcoming Shame and Guilt

1. Acknowledge ADHD as a Legitimate Factor

Admitting that ADHD plays a real role in your life does not excuse mistakes, but it highlights that some aspects of your brain make certain tasks more complicated. This viewpoint can shift blame from "I'm a failure" to "I have a condition that requires different tactics."

2. Practice Self-Talk that is Kinder

If you catch yourself thinking, "I'm useless," or "I can't do anything right," pause. Replace that thought with something balanced like, "I made a mistake because I lost track of the deadline. I can take steps to fix this." Though it might feel odd at first, repeated kinder self-talk can reduce deep shame.

3. Separate Behavior from Self-Worth

When you slip up, say, "That was the wrong action," rather than "I am a worthless person." Focusing on the specific mistake helps you find solutions and avoids attacking your character as a whole.

4. Seek Professional Counseling

A therapist, especially one familiar with adult ADHD, can help you reframe negative thoughts. They might use techniques like cognitive behavioral therapy, guiding you to see patterns in your thinking and teaching healthier responses to guilt triggers.

5. Confide in Safe People

Talking openly with someone who understands ADHD—perhaps a friend, a family member, or a support group—can reduce shame. Hearing them say, "I've been there" or "That is more common than you think" can bring relief and normalize your experience.

Reducing Misunderstandings

1. Educate Key People in Your Life

If you often clash with a partner or boss due to ADHD signs, consider sharing basic information about how ADHD works. This is not about shifting blame but about helping them see you do want to improve. Suggest articles or short videos that explain the condition.

2. Ask Clarifying Questions

If you are unsure what someone expects from you, ask for details. "Could you show me a sample of what you want?" or "When exactly do you need this by?" This level of clarity helps both parties avoid confusion that can lead to accusations later.

3. Use Concrete Communication

When making promises, be specific. Instead of "I'll get this done soon," say "I'll have this finished by Thursday at 3 PM." With clarity, you reduce the chance of letting something slip.

4. Offer Simple Explanations

If you are running late to a friend's event because you lost track of time, you might say, "I apologize. My focus got away from me. I'm working on better reminders." This brief explanation shows respect for the other person's time without a long excuse.

5. Accept That Not Everyone Will Understand

Despite your best efforts, some people will remain skeptical. While it is good to do what you can to clear up misunderstandings, you cannot force everyone to be sympathetic. Learn to let go of those battles and focus on supportive relationships.

Dealing with Outside Judgment

1. Avoid Engaging in Arguments

If a coworker or acquaintance dismisses ADHD as "fake" or "overblown," a heated debate may not change their mind. Often, it is more productive to calmly share a fact or two and move on. Lingering on such arguments can intensify your stress.

2. Draw Boundaries

If someone's comments are hurtful or mocking, set limits. Politely but firmly let them know that such remarks are not acceptable. If they continue, you might reduce contact to protect your well-being.

3. Lean on Allies

When faced with negativity, confiding in supportive friends or family can offset harmful judgments. They can remind you of your strengths or share personal stories of how they have seen you manage challenges.

4. Document Problems at Work

If misunderstandings at your job escalate to the point of harassment or biased treatment, keep records of incidents. Speak to HR or a trusted supervisor. Understanding your rights and the company's policies can help you decide on next steps.

Healthy Responses to Mistakes

1. Own Up Quickly

When a mistake happens, immediately acknowledge it to the relevant person. "I realize I forgot to follow through. I'm sorry, and I'm correcting it now." This direct approach often diffuses tension and shows responsibility.

2. Explain Briefly if Needed

Offer a short explanation if it helps clarify the root cause (e.g., "I overlooked the email in my cluttered inbox"), but do not drag out a long story. People appreciate honesty but do not need every detail.

3. Present a Plan to Fix or Prevent

If possible, include how you will correct the mistake and avoid it next time. For instance, "I've set a daily alarm on my phone so I won't miss these requests in the future."

4. Move Forward

After addressing the slip-up, try not to dwell on it endlessly. Reflection is good, but prolonged shame can trap you in negativity. Learn from it, adjust your strategy, and proceed.

Handling Guilt with Loved Ones

1. Listen to Their Feelings

If your partner or family member is upset by your lapses, let them express it without cutting them off or getting defensive. They need to feel heard.

2. Validate Their Frustration

Even if you disagree with the intensity of their reaction, showing empathy can calm tensions. Say, "I get why you are frustrated. I know my forgetting to call the plumber caused extra hassle."

3. Offer to Make Amends

See if there is a practical way to make the situation better: "I'll handle the phone call tomorrow and cover the extra fee if that helps." This willingness goes a long way toward rebuilding trust.

4. Suggest Joint Solutions

Ask them for input on how both of you can prevent the issue. For example, "Could we keep a shared calendar on the fridge where we write important tasks? That might keep me on track."

5. Resist Self-Punishment

Feeling guilty does not fix the problem if it spirals into self-loathing. Instead, channel that feeling into concrete steps that help ensure the situation does not repeat.

Building Resilience Against Shame

1. Focus on Strengths

Men with ADHD often have bright ideas, strong creativity, and the ability to think outside the box. Recognize these positives. Write them down if needed. Balancing self-criticism with awareness of your good qualities prevents an all-negative mindset.

2. Surround Yourself with Positive Influences

Choose friends, mentors, or support groups that acknowledge ADHD and encourage you. Reduce time spent with people who constantly belittle your struggles or label you in negative ways.

3. Engage in Activities that Boost Confidence

Hobbies or sports you enjoy can restore a sense of competence. Succeeding in an area you care about can counterbalance feelings of inadequacy that arise from ADHD issues.

4. Consider Mindfulness Practices

Short mindfulness sessions—like sitting quietly and noticing your breath—can train you to observe anxious or shame-filled thoughts without letting them control you. Over time, this reduces the emotional punch of negative self-talk.

Using Support Systems

1. Therapy for Deeper Issues

If shame or guilt feel overwhelming, a mental health professional can provide targeted methods. You might explore how childhood experiences shaped your self-image or learn new coping tools.

2. ADHD Support Groups

Meeting others who deal with the same challenges can be a huge relief. Hearing how they handle slip-ups or harsh judgments can spark new ideas. Sharing your own experiences also helps you see you are not alone.

3. Workplace Allies

If you feel comfortable, talking to an HR representative or a trusted supervisor might help. Some workplaces offer accommodations or flexible scheduling for employees with ADHD. Transparency can reduce misunderstandings about performance or behavior.

4. Accountability Partners

Ask a friend or family member if they can be your partner in tackling a recurring issue. For instance, if you tend to miss bill payments, you could both compare notes once a week to ensure everything is in order.

Changing the Inner Script

1. Notice Negative Scripts

Pay attention to how you talk to yourself after a mistake. Do you say, "I always mess up"? That is an exaggerated statement. ADHD might increase the risk of errors, but "always" or "never" are rarely accurate.

2. Practice Balanced Self-Talk

Shift from "I messed up again, I'm hopeless" to "I messed up this time, but I've fixed similar issues before. I can handle it by taking these steps." Keep it grounded in reality.

3. Keep a "Success Log"

Write down daily or weekly successes—finishing a task early, remembering a meeting, or going a whole day without snapping at anyone. These records remind you that, despite flaws, you do achieve many things.

4. Avoid Quick Labels

If you find yourself labeling your behavior with harsh terms, step back. A slip in focus does not equate to being a lazy person. Re-label it as a specific ADHD slip and move on.

The Role of Forgiveness

1. Self-Forgiveness

It is important to forgive yourself for repeated missteps. This does not mean ignoring them, but rather letting go of the emotional baggage that keeps you stuck. A thought like, "I accept that I messed up, and I forgive myself so I can do better," can be freeing.

2. Seeking Forgiveness from Others

If your actions harmed someone, a genuine apology may help them let go of anger or resentment. Focus on sincerity: "I'm sorry for how my forgetfulness affected you. I realize it caused extra stress."

3. Rebuilding Trust Over Time

Forgiveness does not erase consequences. You might need to show consistent improvement to rebuild trust with someone you let down. Patience is key, both for you and for them.

4. Avoid Dwelling on the Past

Once you have apologized or made amends, lingering too long on past errors can trap you in shame. Learn from it, adjust your approach, and put your energy into present actions that reflect your growth.

Handling Cultural or Family Stigma

1. Educate Family or Community

In some cultures, ADHD might be poorly understood. You can share articles or personal stories that explain the condition in simple terms, so relatives see it is not about unwillingness but about brain function.

2. Protect Your Mental Health

If extended family constantly criticizes you, consider setting limits on visits or phone calls. Your well-being should not be sacrificed to fit traditional roles that disregard ADHD.

3. Seek Role Models

Look for men who have ADHD yet function well in your community or similar cultural environment. Their example can inspire you and show family members that success and ADHD are not incompatible.

4. Join Broader Support Groups

If you live in a place with strong stigma, online groups from different regions can offer acceptance you cannot find locally. Over time, these connections might give you the courage to address cultural misunderstandings.

Healing After Long-Term Shame

1. Addressing Childhood Trauma

Some men with ADHD had very harsh school experiences or unsupportive family environments. Therapy can help uncover and heal old wounds that still shape your self-image.

2. Relearning Confidence

You may need to systematically test your abilities in safe ways—taking small risks or starting new habits—so you gather evidence that you can succeed. Each small win rebuilds your sense of capability.

3. Community Involvement

Volunteering or contributing to group activities helps you see your positive impact on others, which weakens the grip of shame. Helping others can also shift the focus from self-criticism to collective progress.

4. Gratitude and Reflection

Spending a few minutes each day thinking about things you are grateful for—your health, a loyal friend, or a chance to learn—can reduce the overshadowing weight of negative self-perception.

Moving Forward with Fewer Misunderstandings

1. Ongoing Education

Learning about ADHD is not a one-time event. Stay updated on research, read personal stories, or listen to experts. The better you understand ADHD, the better you can explain it to others.

2. Improved Communication Skills

Keep working on listening, clarifying, and stating your own needs. Fewer misunderstandings occur if you communicate calmly and precisely. If needed, revisit the tips from earlier chapters on handling conflict.

3. Balanced Accountability

Find a midpoint between blaming ADHD for everything and denying it plays any role. Admit errors, but also know that you must plan to handle them differently next time. That plan might include the tools from earlier chapters—timers, lists, or support groups.

4. Recognize Progress

Each time you bounce back from a mistake without sinking into shame, you are growing. Each successful communication, each well-managed moment of guilt, moves you closer to a healthier relationship with ADHD. Acknowledge these steps, because they show your capability to adapt.

Conclusion of Chapter 17

Shame and guilt can be powerful emotions for men with ADHD, often fueled by repeated mistakes or misunderstandings. While it is natural to feel bad about letting others or yourself down, prolonged shame can trap you in self-doubt, making it even harder to manage ADHD signs. The key is to handle the underlying causes—lack of understanding from others, negative self-talk, and unrealistic standards—and to adopt healthier responses.

Practical strategies like self-forgiveness, focusing on specific errors rather than labeling yourself as a failure, and educating the people around you about ADHD can all lessen shame's impact. Meanwhile, open communication, clear goal-setting, and steady follow-through reduce the misunderstandings that lead to guilt. Remember, ADHD does not define your worth. By learning to navigate shame and guilt constructively, you free up mental energy to manage tasks better and to build stronger relationships, both with yourself and with the people in your life.

Chapter 18: Lifestyle Changes That Make a Difference

Introduction

When someone mentions "lifestyle changes," many think of dieting or adding a quick workout routine. But for men with ADHD, adjusting daily habits can have wide-ranging effects that go beyond physical health. A balanced lifestyle supports mental clarity, emotional stability, and better control of ADHD signs. This chapter explores a range of lifestyle changes that can help you navigate daily tasks, handle stress, and stay focused.

Instead of short-lived efforts, think of these as long-term habits that shape your environment and your body's rhythms. The idea is not to become a perfect health fanatic overnight but to gradually adopt routines that fit your life and make ADHD more manageable. By building on small wins, you can notice improved concentration, steadier moods, and a more organized approach to each day.

Pillars of a Helpful Lifestyle

1. **Structured Routines**: Consistency in sleep, work, and meal times can stabilize the ADHD mind.
2. **Physical Activity**: Regular movement supports brain chemistry that improves focus and mood.
3. **Healthy Eating**: Balanced meals can keep energy steady and reduce crashes that worsen restlessness.
4. **Stress Management**: Finding outlets for stress lowers impulsive reactions and emotional overload.
5. **Positive Relationships**: Healthy social ties motivate better habits and give emotional support.

All these elements work together. For instance, improved nutrition may give you more energy for workouts, which in turn helps you sleep more deeply. Good sleep then helps your brain handle stress and remain focused, reinforcing a positive cycle.

Rethinking Sleep Habits

1. Set a Consistent Bedtime

For men with ADHD, going to bed and waking up at wildly different times can throw off the internal clock. If you can, pick a specific bedtime for weekdays and weekends that does not differ by more than an hour or two. This stability helps regulate energy levels.

2. Create a Bedtime Routine

A simple sequence—like turning off screens 30 minutes before bed, dimming the lights, and reading a physical book—signals your brain that it is time to wind down. This can reduce late-night restlessness or hyperfocus on random tasks.

3. Limit Stimulants Late in the Day

Caffeine in coffee, tea, or energy drinks can linger in your system for hours. If you struggle with falling asleep, try cutting off caffeine by early afternoon. The same goes for nicotine if you smoke or use related products.

4. Address Sleep Disorders

Some men with ADHD experience sleep apnea, restless legs, or other issues. If you suspect a disorder, consider seeing a sleep specialist. Treating it can improve your rest dramatically and may lessen ADHD signs in the daytime.

5. Track Your Progress

You might use a sleep app or just write down your bedtime, wake-up time, and how rested you feel. Over a few weeks, notice patterns. Adjust gradually if you see, for example, that going to bed 30 minutes earlier makes morning routines smoother.

Making Nutrition Work for You

1. Prioritize Steady Energy Foods

Sudden spikes and drops in blood sugar can worsen inattention or irritability. Aim for balanced meals that include protein (chicken, fish, beans) and complex carbs (whole grains, vegetables), rather than sugary snacks or refined white bread.

2. Plan Meals in Advance

If you wait until you are starving, you are more likely to grab junk or skip meals. Setting aside time each weekend to plan or prep a few healthy options can keep you on track. You might cook a big batch of chicken or pasta to portion out for the week.

3. Keep Quick, Nutritious Snacks

Men with ADHD sometimes forget to eat lunch or get stuck in a hyperfocus phase. Having easy snacks like nuts, cheese sticks, yogurt, or fruit helps stabilize your energy when you are busy. This avoids the crash that can come from ignoring hunger for too long.

4. Stay Hydrated

Even mild dehydration affects focus and mood. Keep a water bottle nearby and sip regularly. If plain water bores you, try adding a slice of lemon or cucumber for a subtle flavor boost.

5. Avoid Excessive Sugar and Processed Foods

That quick sugar fix might feel good for a moment, but it can lead to a slump soon after. Heavily processed items—chips, sweet cereals, pastries—lack sustained nutrients. While occasional treats are fine, overdoing these foods can heighten restlessness or lethargy.

The Power of Exercise and Movement

1. Boosting Brain Chemistry

Physical activity releases chemicals in the brain that aid memory, attention, and mood. For some men with ADHD, an energetic workout can calm racing thoughts or reduce fidgety energy.

2. Finding Activities You Enjoy

If you hate running, do not force yourself to do it every day. Explore options: brisk walks, hiking, cycling, swimming, or group sports. The key is to pick something you do not dread, increasing the odds of sticking with it.

3. Short Exercise Breaks

Even brief spurts of movement help if you cannot commit to a full workout. For example, do 10 squats or walk for 5 minutes once every hour. This can break up work sessions, refresh your focus, and give you a small energy boost.

4. Scheduling Workouts

A firm exercise slot in your daily or weekly schedule (like "Workout from 6 PM to 6:30 PM") helps you stay consistent. Setting phone alarms or reminders can keep the plan alive. If possible, work out at a time when your energy is naturally higher—some men prefer mornings, others late afternoon.

5. Exercising with Friends

A buddy system can motivate you to show up and push yourself. You can also combine exercise with socializing, which helps reduce feelings of isolation. For example, joining a basketball pickup game or going on a walking routine with a neighbor can be fun and keep you active.

Managing Stress and Emotional Upset

1. Identify Stressors

Common stressors for men with ADHD include cluttered environments, tight deadlines, and relationship conflicts. Keep a brief log of what stresses you out to see patterns. That awareness helps you plan solutions, such as cleaning your workspace or seeking help before a looming deadline.

2. Explore Relaxation Methods

Deep breathing, gentle stretching, or short mindfulness sessions can lower tension. Some men use guided relaxation apps for a few minutes each morning or night. The goal is not to wipe out all stress but to learn to reset before it piles up.

3. Set Realistic Goals

Overcommitting leads to constant rushing and anxiety. Men with ADHD sometimes say "yes" to too many projects because they feel a burst of excitement at the start. Practice saying "no" or "I'll think about it" to maintain a balanced schedule.

4. Healthy Outlets

Hobbies, journaling, or art can serve as outlets for pent-up emotions. If you feel restless or agitated, channel that energy into something productive or creative, rather than letting it explode in frustration.

5. Seek Professional Help if Needed

If stress or emotional swings become overwhelming, therapy can help you develop coping tools. Medication adjustments might also be considered under a doctor's guidance. It is not a failure to get specialized support; it is a step toward better health.

Simplifying Your Environment

1. Declutter and Organize

Physical clutter can mirror mental clutter. Men with ADHD might benefit from a tidy, simplified living space. If you feel overwhelmed, tackle one small area at a time—a drawer, a closet corner—so you do not give up midway.

2. Labeling Systems

Use labels for shelves or boxes so you know where items go. Color-coding can make it easier to remember. If you have a "keys tray" by the door, you reduce the daily scramble to find your keys.

3. Digital Organization

A messy computer desktop or an overflowing email inbox can contribute to mental fatigue. Spend a bit of time each week cleaning out old messages, creating folders for key categories, and deleting files you no longer need.

4. Limit Unneeded Inputs

Too many background noises—like constant TV or endless phone alerts—can fragment attention. Set your phone to silent or only allow essential notifications during focus times. Keep music or podcasts at a moderate volume if you find them helpful, but avoid overwhelming stimuli.

5. Use Routines for Tidiness

Routine tasks—like doing dishes right after meals or sorting mail each evening—keep messes from building up. By addressing small chores promptly, you avoid big cleanup sessions that can feel too large to handle.

Building Supportive Social Habits

1. Plan Regular Check-Ins with Friends

Loneliness or lack of social contact can worsen ADHD-related stress. Scheduling quick coffee breaks or phone calls with friends ensures you stay connected. This can also help you get feedback on areas you might be struggling with.

2. Family Meetings

If you have a partner or kids, short weekly family meetings can help coordinate tasks, set schedules, and avoid confusion. A big wall calendar can show everyone's commitments, limiting last-minute chaos.

3. Join Groups or Clubs

Whether it is a sports league, a book club, or a community service group, regular gatherings give structure and social interaction. Men with ADHD often thrive in settings that combine shared interests with mild accountability.

4. Lean on Accountability Partners

From the previous chapters, you know accountability can keep you on track. This might mean a friend or coworker who checks in about your progress. Sharing small goals—like finishing a project or cutting back on late-night screen time—can encourage consistent effort.

5. Balance Alone Time and Group Time

Some men with ADHD may swing between craving solitude and seeking social activities. Listen to your personal rhythm. If too much solitude leads to overthinking, try adding more social events. If constant gatherings overwhelm you, set aside quiet hours.

Adjusting Technology Use

1. Screen Time Boundaries

If you find yourself lost in aimless scrolling or gaming, set time limits. Many phones have built-in tools to monitor or restrict app use. If social media is a major distraction, consider logging out during work hours or on weekends.

2. Smartphone-Free Periods

Pick certain times—like meals or the hour before bed—to be phone-free. Put your device on silent and place it away from reach. This break can help your mind relax and improves real-life interactions with people around you.

3. Manage Email and Messaging

Emails and instant messages can pile up. To reduce stress, schedule set times to check them—maybe morning, midday, and late afternoon—rather than responding to each notification in real time. This method frees up longer blocks of focus.

4. Limit Late-Night Technology

Blue light from screens can trick your brain into staying awake. If you must use devices at night, activate the blue light filter or use "night mode." But ideally, read a physical book, journal, or spend time on a calm hobby.

5. Use Tech to Your Advantage

If used wisely, apps can help with to-do lists, reminders, or relaxation. From Chapter 15, you already know about the variety of tools that exist. Combine them with healthy limits so your phone becomes a resource, not a distraction pit.

Tuning Your Work or Study Environment

1. Find the Right Level of Noise

Some men with ADHD thrive in a quiet setting, while others focus better with light background sounds. Experiment with different soundscapes, like instrumental music or white noise. If an office is too quiet, try a low-volume soundtrack. If it is too loud, use noise-cancelling headphones.

2. Break Work into Blocks

Long hours of continuous work can overwhelm ADHD brains. Use techniques such as the Pomodoro Method: focus for 25 minutes, then take a 5-minute break to stretch or grab water. Repeat. These brief intervals often boost productivity.

3. Stand-Up or Movement Options

If you get restless sitting all day, consider a stand-up desk or a small pedal device under your desk. Some workplaces allow walking meetings. These minor changes keep your body engaged, reducing the urge to fidget or daydream.

4. Clear Visual Distractions

If your workspace is cluttered or near high traffic, face your desk away from the door or keep only essential items on the surface. Minimizing triggers in your peripheral vision can help you stay on track.

5. Reward Yourself

When you finish a challenging task, a small reward—like a short walk outside or a healthy snack—can make the process more pleasant. This also links positive feelings to productivity, reinforcing the habit.

Adding Mindfulness or Reflection

1. Morning Check-Ins

Start your day with a one-minute pause: "What is my main task for today?" or "How am I feeling right now?" This helps you set an intention. Some men write it on a sticky note and place it where they can see it.

2. Midday Breathers

A short midday pause—closing your eyes and taking a few slow breaths—resets the mind. This can prevent an afternoon slump or meltdown, especially if you feel stressed.

3. Journaling

Writing a few lines each night about the day's events or your feelings can bring clarity. It also creates a record of patterns in ADHD signs—like times of day you struggle most or emotional triggers that pop up.

4. Gratitude Lists

Write down two or three things you are thankful for every day. This switch in focus from problems to positives can reduce negativity, which in turn can help you stay motivated to maintain healthy routines.

5. Spiritual or Philosophical Practices

If you have a faith tradition or personal philosophy, engaging in daily prayer, quiet reflection, or reading uplifting materials might anchor your mind. The specifics vary, but the goal is a calm mental state.

Tracking Progress

1. Set Measurable Goals

Rather than saying, "I want to get healthier," define clear targets: "Jog twice a week for 20 minutes," or "Drink 6 cups of water daily." This specificity helps you see if you are succeeding or where to tweak.

2. Use a Habit Tracker

Apps or simple charts let you mark each day you complete a desired habit (like going to bed at a certain time). Over weeks, you see a pattern of your consistency, which can encourage you to keep going.

3. Celebrate Small Wins

Every time you hit a milestone—like a month of regular workouts—acknowledge that achievement. A small treat or a note to yourself can keep you invested in the habit. This positive feedback cycle makes it easier to keep going.

4. Reflect on Setbacks

If you fail to keep a routine, do not sink into guilt. Instead, ask, "What caused the slip?" Maybe you scheduled your workout at a time that conflicts with family duties. Identify the barrier, adjust, and move forward.

5. Revisit Goals Regularly

Life changes. You might get a new job, move homes, or add a child to your family. Update your lifestyle targets to match new routines. Staying flexible yet committed will help you maintain healthy habits long-term.

Overcoming Common Hurdles

1. Lack of Motivation

Motivation can come and go, especially if you are dealing with ADHD. On low-motivation days, rely on structure: alarms, pre-made schedules, or accountability from a friend. Consistent routines can carry you through slumps.

2. Time Blindness

Men with ADHD might underestimate how long tasks take. Include buffers in your schedule—plan 30 minutes more than you think you need. This avoids rushing or giving up when tasks extend beyond your guess.

3. Boredom or Restlessness

When a new habit feels dull—like repeating the same workout—change it up. Explore new forms of exercise or a different path for your daily walk. Adding variety can keep you engaged.

4. Overdoing It

Be careful of extremes. If you start a strict diet or an intense daily workout, you might burn out quickly. Begin with modest, achievable changes, and increase only as you adapt.

5. All-or-Nothing Thinking

ADHD can foster the idea that if you fail once, the whole habit is ruined. Instead, treat each day as a fresh start. Missing one workout or having one unhealthy meal does not erase the progress you have already made.

Putting It All Together

1. Start with One Area

Deciding to revamp your sleep, diet, exercise, and stress management all at once can be overwhelming. Pick the area that needs help the most—perhaps sleep. Focus on stabilizing that for a few weeks before adding another change.

2. Use the Tools from Earlier Chapters

Timers, apps, or support groups can help you stay consistent. Remember, it is not about perfection but about building a supportive environment for your ADHD mind.

3. Involve Others

Ask friends or family to join your new habits, like taking an evening walk together or sharing healthy dinner recipes. Social support keeps you accountable and makes the process more fun.

4. Track Small Improvements

Notice if you are waking up less groggy or focusing a bit longer at work. These subtle shifts indicate your lifestyle changes are working. Over time, they can add up to a notable difference in how you feel daily.

5. Adjust as Needed

Life is dynamic. Some changes might not fit your work schedule, or you might develop new interests that change your activity levels. Stay open-minded and keep refining your approach. The goal is to create a daily life that supports your well-being and reduces ADHD hurdles.

Conclusion of Chapter 18

Lifestyle changes can go beyond surface-level wellness for men with ADHD, helping to stabilize moods, sharpen focus, and reduce disorganization. By improving sleep, fine-tuning diet, adding regular movement, and managing stress, you create an environment where ADHD signs can be less disruptive. Simple steps—like sticking to a consistent bedtime, using short breaks during work, or having well-balanced meals—are often the foundation.

The best approach is gradual, realistic, and tailored to your daily life. Extreme overhauls might lead to quick burnout. Instead, adopt or refine one habit at a time until it feels natural, then move on to the next. Along the way, track progress, adapt to new situations, and remain patient if setbacks occur. Over months and years, these lifestyle adjustments can form a strong support system for your ADHD management, letting you face tasks, relationships, and personal goals with more clarity and calm.

Chapter 19: Sorting Out Myths from Reality

Introduction

ADHD has attracted many myths over the years. Some people think it is merely an excuse for laziness or that it disappears after childhood. Others believe medication is the only solution or that people with ADHD cannot succeed in demanding fields. These misunderstandings make it harder for men with ADHD to get proper help and acceptance.

In this chapter, we explore typical myths about ADHD, explain the truth behind each one, and look at why these myths continue to exist. We also discuss how to respond when you hear false claims, whether from family, friends, or coworkers. By learning the facts, you can stand up for yourself or others in a calm, clear way. Awareness of these truths can also keep you from internalizing negative messages that block your progress.

Why Myths Persist

1. Lack of Awareness

ADHD has not always been widely recognized or studied. Because it was misunderstood for a long time, many older beliefs linger, especially in places where mental health topics are not openly discussed.

2. Media Portrayals

Television or movies might show characters with ADHD as simply hyper kids or disorganized adults who cannot do anything right. These portrayals can shape public opinion, creating stereotypes that do not reflect the varied signs of ADHD.

3. Oversimplification

The brain is complex, and ADHD signs vary from person to person. People searching for easy explanations might latch onto a single cause—like "bad parenting" or "too much sugar"—which ignores the scientific findings about how genes and brain chemistry matter.

4. Confusion with Normal Behavior

Some critics say ADHD is not real because "everyone has trouble focusing sometimes." This overlooks the difference in severity and frequency. People with ADHD see these struggles daily, affecting work, relationships, and well-being.

5. Mixed Experiences with Medication

When one person has a bad experience with ADHD medication, they might assume all treatments fail or are harmful. They may spread this view, ignoring the fact that many people respond well to a range of treatment options.

Myth 1: "ADHD Only Affects Children"

The Claim

Many assume ADHD is a childhood issue. They believe that once a person becomes an adult, the problem ends—or that if the child is not bouncing off walls, ADHD must be gone.

Reality

- **Continuing Signs**: Research shows that many children with ADHD continue to have signs into adulthood. Some men only learn they have ADHD after facing repeated problems on the job or in personal life.

- **Changing Appearance of Signs**: Hyperactivity might lessen with age, but inattention or impulsivity can stay. Adults may appear restless internally or switch jobs often instead of running around like a hyper child.
- **Missed Diagnoses**: Some men were never diagnosed as kids. They managed to get by in school, only to find real challenges in adult settings where tasks are less structured.

How to Respond: If someone says ADHD is just for kids, explain that while signs often appear in youth, many adults continue to struggle. Offer examples of how focus issues and impulsive actions can show up differently in an adult's routine.

Myth 2: "ADHD Is Not a Real Condition"

The Claim

Some people say ADHD is made up, a modern excuse for undisciplined behavior. They question if there is real science behind it.

Reality

- **Documented by Medical Organizations**: Groups like the American Psychiatric Association and the World Health Organization recognize ADHD as a valid condition. It is described in diagnostic manuals used worldwide.
- **Brain Research**: Studies using brain scans and neuropsychological tests find differences in structure, activity, and chemical balance in people with ADHD.
- **Genetic Links**: ADHD tends to run in families. While it is not purely genetic, a strong hereditary aspect is often found.

How to Respond: If someone doubts ADHD's validity, you can mention that major health agencies and scientific research confirm its existence. Also, mention how treatment—both medication and therapy—often leads to tangible improvements, which would not happen if it was not a genuine condition.

Myth 3: "ADHD Means Low Intelligence"

The Claim

A common misconception is that men with ADHD are less clever. They assume trouble focusing equals a lack of ability to understand or learn.

Reality

- **Intelligence Varies**: ADHD does not indicate low or high intelligence; it affects attention and impulse control, not raw mental capacity. People with ADHD can be very bright or struggle, just like anyone else.
- **Underperformance**: Because of disorganization or time-management issues, some men with ADHD do poorly in school or at work, giving the false impression of lower intelligence. In reality, with correct support, many excel.
- **Examples of Success**: There are stories of well-known individuals with ADHD—entrepreneurs, scientists, athletes—who have achieved major goals. Their success shows that intelligence is not diminished by ADHD.

How to Respond: Point out that ADHD affects how the brain processes tasks, not how smart a person is. Emphasize that with coping methods, many men with ADHD show the same range of intelligence as the general population.

Myth 4: "ADHD Is Caused by Bad Parenting or Weak Will"

The Claim

Some people claim ADHD arises from weak discipline at home or a lazy approach to life. They see signs like restlessness or inattention as proof that parents did not teach their child properly.

Reality

- **Neurobiological Roots**: While environment plays a role in any child's behavior, ADHD is primarily linked to brain pathways involving attention and impulse control. Parenting style cannot create ADHD out of thin air.
- **Effort Does Not Erase It**: Many men with ADHD work extremely hard to organize themselves. The condition is not about lack of willpower. Even with strong effort, certain tasks remain tricky without targeted strategies or treatments.
- **Parenting Approaches**: Good parenting can help a child with ADHD manage signs, but it cannot simply make it vanish. The condition involves deeper brain mechanisms that need structure, therapy, or medication.

How to Respond: When someone blames ADHD on bad parenting, mention the scientific agreement that ADHD stems from brain-related factors. Add that even well-structured households can have children with ADHD, proving it is not a simple parenting flaw.

Myth 5: "Medication Is the Only Option"

The Claim

Others believe the only way to handle ADHD is by taking medication, usually stimulants. They might also say medication will "fix" everything or that it is dangerous and should never be used.

Reality

- **Different Treatments**: While medication can help many, it is not the sole approach. Therapy, coaching, lifestyle changes, and support systems also play vital roles. Some men with ADHD find certain non-stimulant medications or counseling more useful.
- **Individual Differences**: Not everyone reacts the same way to medication. One man might see a major boost in focus, while another sees little improvement or more side effects. Personalization is key.
- **Multimodal Approach**: Combining medication with behavioral strategies often gives better results than either alone. Tools like planners, timers, or group therapy can address daily challenges that pills alone may not fix.

How to Respond: If you hear that ADHD can "only" be helped by medication or that medication is always bad, explain that treatment varies widely. Share that many use a combination of methods—therapy, lifestyle adjustments, coaching—to address different aspects of ADHD.

Myth 6: "ADHD People Are Just Lazy"

The Claim

Because men with ADHD sometimes have trouble starting or finishing tasks, outsiders may label them as lazy, assuming they just do not want to try.

Reality

- **Task Initiation Problems**: Starting a task can be extra tough for ADHD brains because the reward circuits might need stronger stimulation. It is not about not wanting to do it; it is about how the brain processes motivation.
- **Hyperfocus vs. Disinterest**: Men with ADHD might work extremely hard if the topic interests them. When the task feels boring, they

struggle, which can look like laziness. In truth, it is a mismatch in how their attention system is triggered.
- **Daily Effort**: Many men with ADHD put in huge effort just to keep up with daily tasks—maintaining schedules, paying bills on time, remembering appointments. Calling them lazy overlooks this hidden work.

How to Respond: Clarify that ADHD often includes a mismatch between the brain's reward system and typical tasks. Remind skeptics that calling men with ADHD lazy ignores the real challenges and often the unseen effort they make every day.

Myth 7: "ADHD People Cannot Hold Complex or Demanding Jobs"

The Claim

People think men with ADHD cannot handle high-level careers that require organization, detail management, or steady routines.

Reality

- **Variety of Strengths**: Many men with ADHD thrive in jobs that involve creativity, quick decision-making, or hands-on tasks. Others manage demanding roles by using tools and support systems.
- **Compensation Methods**: With routines, planners, or coaching, men with ADHD can excel in administrative or detail-heavy jobs as well. They learn to offset weaknesses with practical steps, sometimes performing better than average.
- **Examples of Success**: There are surgeons, pilots, business leaders, and others with ADHD who succeed. The condition requires adjustments, but it does not bar a person from any field if they have the interest and the right support.

How to Respond: Note that ADHD does not lock someone out of a career. Different roles might better match personal strengths, but many men with ADHD do well in both creative and structured fields once they find ways to stay organized and focused.

Myth 8: "ADHD Is Caused by Too Much Screen Time or Video Games"

The Claim

Because children and adults these days spend hours on screens, some say ADHD is caused by digital overload.

Reality

- **Pre-Existing Traits**: ADHD can make a person seek stimulation, so they might gravitate toward video games or social media. The screen time is often a result of ADHD, not the sole cause.
- **Environmental Factors**: Excessive screen time might worsen signs like inattention, but it does not create ADHD from nothing. If someone already has ADHD, they might fall deeper into screens as a coping mechanism.
- **Balance Matters**: Limiting screen time can help manage ADHD, but saying it is the root cause overlooks the real neurological basis.

How to Respond: Emphasize that while too much screen use can feed inattention issues or disrupt healthy routines, ADHD is a broader condition that exists regardless of whether someone is glued to a phone or not.

Myth 9: "Only Boys or Men Show Hyperactivity"

The Claim

Some believe that ADHD is mostly found in boys, with the main sign being obvious hyperactivity. They say girls or women rarely have it, so if an adult woman is calm, she cannot have ADHD.

Reality

- **Different Sign Profiles**: Women or girls with ADHD often show more inattentive signs—daydreaming, quiet distraction—rather than loud restlessness. This can lead to missed diagnoses.
- **Men with Less Hyperactivity**: Even among men, not everyone is hyperactive. Some might mainly face inattention or internal restlessness, which is not as visible.
- **Undiagnosed Women**: Because of this myth, many females are not diagnosed until adulthood. They struggled silently, overshadowed by the image of the "loud, hyper boy."

How to Respond: If you hear someone say ADHD only shows up in hyper boys, explain that the condition has multiple sign types. Some men and many women have "quiet" or inattentive forms, which are just as valid.

Myth 10: "ADHD Goes Away if You Just Try Harder"

The Claim

Some people suggest that ADHD is a motivation problem. They believe if the person only put in enough effort, they would not have issues.

Reality

- **Brain Wiring**: Motivation alone cannot correct differences in how signals move in the ADHD brain. Trying harder helps to a point, but it does not remove the executive function challenges.
- **Stress from Overcompensation**: Some men burn out by pushing themselves relentlessly to keep up. Without appropriate tools or treatments, "trying harder" can lead to anxiety, exhaustion, or mental health problems.
- **Need for Specific Strategies**: Real improvements come from combining personal effort with proven methods—like structured routines, medication (when appropriate), therapy, or coaching.

How to Respond: Highlight that while effort does matter, telling someone with ADHD to "just try harder" is like telling someone with poor vision to "just see better." Tools, strategies, and sometimes medication are needed for consistent results.

Combating Myths in Everyday Life

1. Educate Yourself Deeply

Knowledge is power. Keep up with reliable information—medical websites, books by experts, or support groups—for facts and research findings.

2. Practice a Quick Explanation

If you run into repeated myths, have a short explanation ready. For example, "ADHD is a real condition that affects focus and self-control. Science shows it is linked to brain pathways, not laziness."

3. Share Personal Experiences Wisely

Sometimes, sharing your own challenges—and solutions—can change how someone views ADHD. Real-life stories often stick more than abstract details. However, only share what you are comfortable revealing.

4. Encourage Others to Seek Sources

If a boss or friend clings to a myth, suggest they look at official health sites or talk with a mental health professional. Shift the argument from you vs. them to them exploring objective data.

5. Know When to Walk Away

Not everyone wants to learn. If the other person refuses to listen or uses insults, you are not obligated to keep debating. Protect your energy and move on.

Moving Past Myths in Your Own Mind

1. Challenge Internalized Misconceptions

You may have absorbed negative beliefs—such as "I'm just lazy" or "I can't be successful." Actively question these thoughts. Remember what experts and your own achievements show: ADHD is real and does not define your abilities.

2. Remind Yourself of Facts

If you feel guilty or incompetent, recall the factual basis of ADHD. It is not a moral failing. Your struggles have scientific explanations, and workable solutions exist.

3. Watch Out for All-or-Nothing Thinking

Myths often feed black-and-white views—like "Either I fix ADHD completely or I fail." In reality, ADHD management is a continuous process with ups and downs.

4. Celebrate Each Progress Marker

When you spot even small improvements—like finishing a task on time or politely correcting someone's misunderstanding—note it. These achievements counteract the harmful myths that claim you cannot progress.

5. Seek Support

If you find certain myths weighing on you, talk them through with a therapist, coach, or supportive friend. Hearing an outside perspective can break the loop of negative thoughts.

The Bigger Picture: Why Correcting Myths Matters

1. Better Self-Esteem

When men with ADHD know the truth, they stop punishing themselves for signs they cannot fully control. This knowledge fosters a healthier sense of self-worth and reduces the shame that myths tend to create.

2. Improved Relationships

Friends, partners, and coworkers who understand ADHD can adapt expectations and provide the right kind of support, leading to less conflict.

3. More Productive Work Environments

When employers grasp that ADHD is real, they may allow flexible scheduling, use productivity tools, or offer quiet spaces. These accommodations can enhance performance and job satisfaction.

4. Less Social Stigma

As more people learn the facts, society can move away from labeling men with ADHD as lazy or disruptive. This lowers the stigma and encourages more men to seek diagnosis or help without feeling judged.

5. Better Research and Policies

If the public rejects myths and accepts scientific findings, there may be more funding for ADHD research, better insurance coverage for treatments, and improved support systems in schools and workplaces.

Overcoming Myth Barriers in Various Settings

At Home

- **Open Dialogue**: Have ongoing talks with family or roommates about ADHD and how it shows up for you.
- **Shared Learning**: Invite them to read an article or watch a short video about ADHD together, then discuss.
- **Plan Solutions**: If certain myths lead to friction, propose a fix. For example, if they think you "just do not care," show them the scheduling steps you are taking.

At Work

- **Educate HR or Supervisors**: If you choose to disclose ADHD, offer clear, concise info on how it affects your job performance and the accommodations that help you thrive.
- **Peer Communication**: If coworkers make offhand remarks based on myths, gently correct them if you feel safe. Keep it professional and focused on the facts.
- **Use Resources**: If your company has an employee assistance program, see if they offer ADHD support or education.

In Social Circles

- **Address Jokes**: Sometimes, friends or acquaintances joke about ADHD in a dismissive way. Decide if you want to correct them politely.
- **Lead by Example**: Show that you manage ADHD proactively, whether through using apps, note-taking, or other methods, so they see you are serious about your condition.
- **Introduce Them to Success Stories**: If they doubt men with ADHD can succeed, mention famous innovators, athletes, or professionals who have ADHD and still reach their goals.

Conclusion of Chapter 19

Myths about ADHD often create barriers, fueling shame, confusion, or unfair judgments. For men with ADHD, learning and sharing the actual facts can break these barriers. From the false idea that ADHD ends with childhood to the claim that it results from bad parenting, each myth misses the truth about how this condition really works. Recognizing the genuine science and the variety of experiences helps everyone—men with ADHD and their families, coworkers, or communities—move forward more cooperatively.

It is normal to feel irritated or discouraged by these myths. But equipping yourself with accurate information and a calm way to present it can make a big difference. Addressing myths helps you defend your self-esteem, secure the accommodations or support you need, and educate those around you. Over time, open conversations rooted in facts can reduce stigma and free men with ADHD from stereotypes, allowing them to concentrate on personal development instead of fighting constant misconceptions.

Chapter 20: Summary and Ongoing Growth

Introduction

You have reached the final chapter of this book about men with ADHD—its challenges, solutions, and the path toward a more balanced life. Throughout these pages, we have covered how ADHD can appear in men, the ways it affects work or personal life, and methods for coping. We have explored therapy, medicine, money management, relationships, and many other topics. Now, it is time to bring everything together.

This concluding chapter offers a big-picture review of the main points and provides guidance on how to keep progressing. ADHD does not vanish with a single treatment or a short program. It is an ongoing process of learning, adapting, and occasionally stumbling. The difference now is that you have a toolbox of strategies and an informed perspective. By blending what you have learned with your own experiences, you can continue to refine how you handle ADHD for years to come.

Major Lessons from the Book

1. ADHD Is Real and Manageable

You have learned that ADHD is not a sign of laziness or low intelligence. It is a valid condition linked to how the brain handles focus, impulse control, and daily organization. Men with ADHD do face certain obstacles, but these are not insurmountable.

2. Signs Vary Among Individuals

Some men show more restlessness and impulsivity, while others mainly have inattentive signs. In adulthood, hyperactivity may be quieter, expressed as internal agitation or job-hopping. Personalizing how you tackle these signs is key—no single approach fits everyone.

3. Diagnosis Opens Doors

Getting a formal evaluation can reduce confusion, allowing you to pinpoint why certain struggles have persisted. A clear diagnosis means you can access relevant therapies, supports, or accommodations at work and school.

4. Treatment Options Are Diverse

Medication helps many, but it is not the only route. Therapy styles—like cognitive behavioral therapy or coaching—offer practical ways to manage thoughts and habits. Tools like planners, digital apps, or support groups help handle daily tasks. Lifestyle adjustments—exercise, good sleep, stress control—amplify all other efforts.

5. Relationships Need Understanding

Whether with a partner, children, or coworkers, men with ADHD often need to work on communication, conflict handling, and routine sharing. Openness about ADHD and willingness to adjust expectations can strengthen connections, reducing friction and resentment.

6. Emotions and Self-Image Matter

Shame, guilt, or feeling "less than" are common. Recognizing that ADHD factors into these emotions lets you address them with the right coping methods. Self-forgiveness and balanced self-talk help you stay motivated instead of feeling trapped by mistakes.

7. Myths Are Harmful

False beliefs—like "ADHD is not real" or "It ends in childhood"—distort how people see men with ADHD and how men see themselves. Armed with facts, you can stand up to these myths, whether they come from outside sources or your own self-doubt.

8. Growth Is Ongoing

ADHD management is not a one-and-done event. Life stages shift, new challenges arise, and you must adapt. This is normal, not a sign of failure. Staying flexible and keeping your methods up to date allows you to handle fresh obstacles with confidence.

Building a Long-Term Plan

1. Identify Your Core Goals

Reflect: what are the top priorities for the next six months or year? It might be improving work performance, strengthening a relationship, or cutting down on impulsive spending. Focusing on a few major goals helps you direct your energy.

2. Choose Methods That Fit

From the many strategies presented—therapy, medication, scheduling tools, exercise routines—pick what aligns best with your daily rhythm. If you are short on time, perhaps start with a single technique like a monthly budget system or a daily to-do app.

3. Create Simple Metrics

Check your progress in concrete ways. For instance, if your goal is to reduce late bill payments, count how many times you pay on time each month. If you aim to lower impulsive outbursts at home, track how many heated conflicts happen per week. Seeing numbers or simple tallies can be motivating.

4. Schedule Checkpoints

Put reminders in your planner or phone—maybe every month—to review how you are doing. Ask yourself: "Am I meeting my core goals? Which strategies are working? Which are not?" This self-check prevents drifting back to old habits unnoticed.

5. Be Ready to Adjust

If something is not working, do not label yourself a failure. Tweak the plan. Perhaps try a different tool, speak to a therapist about a new approach, or get feedback from a mentor or accountability buddy. This flexible mindset avoids the trap of quitting at the first setback.

Strengthening Personal Habits

1. Refine Your Routines

Consistent routines reduce mental effort. If you already have a morning schedule, check if you can add something small—like a quick planning session for the day. If bedtime is chaotic, incorporate steps like dimming lights or reading a physical book.

2. Keep the Physical Space Orderly

You do not have to be a neat freak, but some level of organization helps prevent lost items or missed documents. Regularly purge clutter and store important things in labeled spots.

3. Use Reminders Before Big Events

Whether it is a work deadline or a family gathering, set multiple alarms or notifications leading up to it. Men with ADHD sometimes forget until the last second. Gentle nudges spaced out over days or hours help you prepare calmly.

4. Limit Tempting Distractions

If you know that social media or certain games eat your time, use app blockers during work hours or keep the phone away when focusing. Some men find success by removing tempting icons from the phone's home screen, forcing them to think twice before opening them.

5. Practice Mindful Choices

When you feel an urge—like buying a flashy new gadget or skipping a chore—pause. Ask yourself, "Is this action helpful for my overall goals?" This brief moment of reflection can prevent impulsive decisions that lead to regret later.

Maintaining Healthy Relationships

1. Continue Open Communication

Do not assume your partner or close friends remember everything about your ADHD. Periodically share updates: "I am trying a new approach with budgeting—if I seem stressed, that is why." Such directness helps them support you.

2. Give and Receive Feedback

If a loved one points out you are slipping in some routine, try not to become defensive. Use it as data: "Thanks for letting me know; I will check my reminders." Likewise, gently request feedback on how you are doing, focusing on progress rather than perfection.

3. Set Shared Goals

For men with ADHD who have families, consider forming joint objectives—like family budgeting, weekly meal planning, or specific times for shared leisure. This reduces confusion over who does what, easing tension in daily life.

4. Respect Others' Boundaries

Loved ones can also get overwhelmed. If they ask for space or want to handle some tasks alone, respect that. Balancing your ADHD-driven need for help with their personal limits keeps relationships healthy.

5. Seek Counseling if Needed

Couples therapy or family counseling can help if repeated conflicts arise around ADHD-related habits. A neutral professional can mediate, offer strategies, and ensure everyone feels heard.

Career and Financial Stability

1. Keep Improving Work Skills

Look for small courses or workshops—time management, public speaking, or project planning. Each new skill can offset ADHD challenges in the workplace. If cost is an issue, some are offered free online or through local community centers.

2. Monitor Job Fit

If you feel stuck in a job that clashes severely with your ADHD profile, consider if a different role might suit you better. Some men with ADHD excel in creative or active jobs, while others manage well in structured environments with the right supports.

3. Regular Money Check-Ins

Money management does not run on autopilot. Even after setting a budget, review it monthly or weekly. Are you impulsively spending again? Did you forget a bill? Use apps or accountability partners to stay on track.

4. Negotiate Accommodations

If your workplace has an HR department, see if they can provide slight schedule flexibility or a quiet space. Some men do not want to disclose ADHD, which is a personal choice. But if you do, showing an HR rep how a minor tweak can boost your productivity might be worthwhile.

5. Plan for Long-Term Goals

A steady job is not enough. Think about retirement savings or paying off debts. Men with ADHD sometimes avoid future planning because it feels abstract. Use automatic transfers into a savings account, or set up a debt snowball plan so these goals progress without needing constant reminders.

Emotional Health and Self-Reflection

1. Watch for Burnout

If you notice extreme fatigue, irritability, or apathy, you may be pushing too hard. Scale back, rest, or talk to a therapist. Men with ADHD can accidentally take on too much, chasing stimulation until they collapse.

2. Continue Therapy or Support Group

Even if you have made gains, staying in a support group or occasional therapy can keep you grounded. You might not need weekly sessions, but a monthly or quarterly check-in helps you avoid slipping into old patterns.

3. Practice Self-Compassion

Mistakes will happen. When they do, avoid harsh self-criticism. Remind yourself you have ADHD, that slip-ups are part of learning, and that you have the tools to fix the situation. This mindset helps you bounce back quickly.

4. Celebrate Small Victories

Notice every time you complete tasks on time, handle a conflict calmly, or remember an appointment without last-minute panic. These mini-wins show you are growing. Acknowledge them to keep your morale high.

5. Balance Solitude and Social Input

Everybody needs a certain mix of alone time and social contact. Find what recharges you best. Too much isolation can worsen inattention or sadness, while too many social events might lead to stress. Adjust your schedule until you find a healthy middle ground.

Adapting to Life Transitions

1. Changes in Roles

Marriage, parenthood, or a new job can shift your daily structure. Revisit your ADHD strategies when major transitions occur. Ask your partner or loved ones to help you adapt to new routines.

2. Aging with ADHD

Older men sometimes notice changes in hormone levels, energy, or memory. If you see changes in how ADHD signs appear, talk to a doctor. Adjusting medication or trying new coping strategies can help you navigate aging.

3. Addressing Shifting Goals

What you wanted at 25 might differ at 45. If your life direction changes—like launching a business or traveling more—re-examine how ADHD fits. You might need fresh organizational methods for new challenges.

4. Passing Skills to Children

If you have kids, especially if they show ADHD patterns, share the strategies you have learned. This can prevent them from feeling isolated or doomed to struggle. Your own experience can help them handle signs earlier and more effectively.

5. Staying Flexible

Life rarely remains static. By keeping a flexible viewpoint—ready to swap out an old system for a new one when needed—you remain resilient. ADHD thrives on adaptability; if you remain open to adjusting, you will continue to improve.

Keeping Your Momentum

1. Check In with Yourself Regularly

A simple monthly ritual: "What is working well? What is my biggest ADHD-related challenge right now? Which strategy can I try next?" Writing this down or talking it through with a friend stops ADHD from drifting into chaos.

2. Maintain Good Habits

Sleep, food, exercise, stress management—these are the foundation. If you skip these basics, other plans might crumble. Keep the lifestyle changes from Chapter 18 in mind as daily pillars.

3. Seek New Information

The field of ADHD research continues to evolve. New apps, therapies, or coaching techniques pop up. Stay alert to updates. If something resonates with you, consider giving it a fair try.

4. Build a Support Network

From Chapter 16, recall the importance of people around you—family, friends, professionals. Keep that network active. Expand it if necessary. Knowing you have folks to lean on can prevent small troubles from becoming major crises.

5. Acknowledge Your Progress

Take a moment—weekly, monthly—to note the positive strides you have made. Did you hold a job for longer than before? Did you finish a big project on time? Recognizing improvements fuels the motivation to keep refining your ADHD management.

Addressing Potential Setbacks

1. Relapses Happen

You might face a rough patch: missed deadlines, friction with a partner, or financial slip-ups. Instead of panicking, see these events as signals that your current methods need a tune-up.

2. Revisit Basics

If you are overwhelmed, go back to fundamental steps: checking your daily routine, adjusting sleep, or reintroducing a scheduling app. Often, returning to these core habits stabilizes you quickly.

3. Ask for Guidance

If you are stuck, do not wait to reach out. A therapist, support group, or even a close friend can offer a fresh viewpoint. The earlier you seek help, the less time you spend in a cycle of mistakes.

4. Consider Medication Reevaluation

If you are on ADHD medication and it suddenly feels less effective, consult your doctor. Tolerance, life stress, or aging might require dose tweaks or even switching medication.

5. Keep Trying

Sometimes, you might get discouraged. Remember, ADHD is a long-term condition. A short slump does not wipe out all the gains you have made. Persistence is often the deciding factor between reverting to old patterns and moving forward again.

Looking Ahead: A Broader Perspective

1. Advocacy and Awareness

As you learn to handle ADHD better, you might feel inspired to help others. Sharing your story or supporting advocacy groups can ease the road for men who are newly diagnosed or feeling isolated.

2. Breaking Stigma in Your Circles

If you feel comfortable, educate people in your community—schools, workplaces, or social groups. Encouraging open discussions about ADHD can improve acceptance and reduce harmful myths.

3. Supporting Future Generations

Whether you have children or nieces/nephews, showing them that ADHD can be managed sends a vital message. They grow up seeing that, while ADHD may present some hurdles, it also comes with creativity and unique ideas.

4. Setting Bigger Goals

Once basic ADHD signs are under better control, you can aim for goals you might have once dismissed—starting a side business, volunteering more, writing a book, or acquiring new skills. Freed from constant chaos, you may find new opportunities.

5. Celebrating Personal Growth

Remember how far you have come. Each skill you have learned—time blocking, respectful conflict resolution, budgeting—reflects real progress. Even if you are not perfect, you have grown. Recognizing that allows you to keep building on your strong points.

Final Encouragement

Men with ADHD often feel that the world moves in a different rhythm, making it hard to keep up. Yet you are not alone. Many men have faced similar trials and found ways to shine. By diagnosing ADHD accurately, building supportive routines, and staying open to adjustments, you can transform those difficulties into clearer roads for productivity, stable relationships, and personal satisfaction.

Remember, this book has presented a wide range of topics, from money handling to fatherhood, from emotional health to workplace success. You do not have to master it all right away. Pick the areas that resonate most or cause you the biggest headaches. Start there, use the tips, and experiment with tweaks until you see improvement. Then, move on to the next item on your list.

The most important takeaway is that ADHD does not define your worth or limit your ability to lead a fulfilling life. It is a condition you can manage with awareness, effort, and a system of tools that match your personal style. You have read about various methods, from therapy to technology, from lifestyle changes to relationship advice. These can be mixed and matched, tested, and refined. Over time, you will discover a personal strategy that works for you. With every hurdle you clear, you build confidence and gain momentum.

So, as you close this book, keep your mind open to future learning. Stay in tune with how your ADHD signs shift over time, keep an eye out for fresh resources or support networks, and never hesitate to seek help if you feel stuck. Each chapter you have read is a stepping stone, giving you knowledge to tackle ADHD with greater skill. This is not the end of your story, but a solid foundation. Move forward with the understanding that progress is possible, setbacks are temporary, and your life can be shaped to suit not just ADHD's demands, but your own hopes and aspirations. You hold the pen for the next chapter—write it in a way that respects your needs, talents, and growth.

www.ingramcontent.com/pod-product-compliance
Lightning Source LLC
LaVergne TN
LVHW012043070526
838202LV00056B/5575